From T

John James

This book is dedicated to those still in the darkness

Acknowledgments

There are many people I need to thank. Thank you to Wayne Samuel for your friendly ear, your patience and your honesty. I would like to thank GPs Doctor Corbitt and Emma for their help and advice as well as their deep understanding, kindness and sensitivity. Thank you to Victim Support, Worcester especially for their support and giving me someone to offload onto without judgment. Thank you to Men's Advice Line just for listening. A huge thanks to Let's Talk who got the tears flowing and opened up my emotions so that I may heal. To the wise and inspiring men I met in India and Nepal, Bijaya Ghimire, Dipesh Chapagain and Farid Baig, thank you so much, we are family of the soul. Thank you to the Boudha Inn Meditation Center, Kathmandu, Nepal, you changed my life and I will be forever grateful.

Thank you to Lisa Ventura and also to Patricia Camp, without your guidance this project may have never reached completion.

I would like to thank ManKind Initiative, who have supported this project, and to the bands Nazareth and Thunder for their support and best wishes. To all the bands whose music I've used to help me tell this story, I thank you for the inspiration that you have given, not only in this instance, but throughout my life.

I reserve my biggest thank you for last. Thank you to my ex-wife Lizzie, there are a million reasons you should have walked away, but you're still in my life and we remained friends and I thank the universe for that.

Disclaimer

Though I have tried to be as truthful as possible, a few details have had to be changed. Several details have been changed to fall in line with the confidentiality policy I adhere to, as I work in the care sector. The timeline within these pages may differ from the actual timeline of the events, this is used to tighten up the narrative, as the inclusion of every minor, insignificant detail would bore you, however, the events themselves are factual.

Finally, the names of some of the people mentioned have been changed.

Thank you

John James

Also by the author

Unnatural Selection

The Rose

Pandora's Kiss (coming soon)

Voices From The Dark (coming 2019)

"Once upon a time I was falling in love
But now I'm only falling apart
And there's nothing I can do
A total eclipse of the heart"

Bonnie Tyler

Note from the author

No, this is not a story in which I play the part of an innocent victim and ask for your sympathy. I was never innocent, in fact, I have gone through many years of not being a nice person at all, not violent, I have never been a violent person, but I have been selfish, egotistical and I am certainly guilty of being stupid. I have also been an angry person, not violent as I have said, but angry; I have been angry about everything and played the part of a victim many times too and this journey that you are about to read, has taught me as much about my wrong doings as those of other people. So, no, I don't want you to see me as innocent. I don't want your sympathy, I don't want you to feel sorry for me, I'm not asking that you even like me. All I ask is that you read this and try to understand what went on and how, maybe, you can learn from my experience and incorporate it into your life.

Needless to say, that when writing this I had to re-live my past. I had to think about things I'd not thought about in a long time and, in doing so, I had to decide how to present the facts to you, the reader. It is an unpleasant read I feel, if the reader is constantly faced with the sentence, 'little was I to know' – that injection of hindsight. As you have no such hindsight when you are actually going through whatever you go through, I decided to eliminate this as much as I could. I decided to write events as they were, that is to say, without hindsight, as if I have no knowledge of what was to come. This way, I have attempted to reflect my true feelings, be they feelings of love, guilt, anger or depression, as they occurred. Taking into account that each of the events I talk about were experienced while in the throes of sometimes powerful emotions, I have pieced together my recollections the best I could trying to be as honest and forthright as possible.

That honesty does not start and end with the recollections of others, but also of myself. I would not think it fair, to tell the story of others and pick and choose at the truths about me. I have opened myself up to you and have been vulnerable in my honesty. Some of which I am about to tell you does not reflect favourably on me and sometimes it's just downright embarrassing, but, hey, if I'm going to tell the truth I may as well tell it. The whole truth and nothing but the truth so help me.

Although my story involves abuse, it is not a story of abuse; it is the story of a journey that includes much more than that. This is a story of love and hate and of cruelty, but also of passion; it is a story of mental illness, fear and darkness, but also of peace and light and of happiness. It is a story that has taken me back to painful memories, back to the time of love and betrayal, of words like daggers and of magical moments that make me smile.

And so, I hand my life over to you. Please read on with an open mind and an open heart.

Peace

John James

"It's like an infection

It's a disease

But no reflection

It's gonna make your blood freeze"

Motorhead

I felt the presence before I had even opened my eyes, something malevolent entering the bedroom. I whimpered beneath my breath trying not to move, not to give any signs that I was aware of its presence. My heart was beating so strongly in my chest that I could hear the rush of blood in my ears and feared that it would be audible to whatever was now closing in on my still form.

I swallowed hard trying to decide what I should do, should I fight or try to escape, but how could I? It was in between me and the door and it would be on top of me soon as I felt its weight on the edge of the bed.

I took a deep breath and counted to three silently to myself. At once I turned, my hands coming up to protect me from any attack.

In the pale moonlight I saw her, Monica, my now ex-girlfriend. Her eyes were black as midnight, her mouth twisted in a villainous snarl. Her arms were raised above her head and grasped between her gnarled hands was a large kitchen knife.

I tried to move, to escape the descending blade but something held me in place, an invisible weight on my chest. I raised my hands, but the knife passed through them as if they were mere apparitions and she plunged the blade into my chest. As my mouth opened in a silent scream, the sound taken from me by the shock of pain, she ripped the knife from my chest and plunged it in again, and then again, and again. Blood splashed across her demon-like features and I swore I heard her laugh.

I shocked awake, my hand grasping at my chest, tears already in my eyes, the picture of Monica's face burning in my head, the stain of the nightmare infecting my waking mind.

I half fell out of bed and stumbled from my bedroom and to the door of my flat. I flung it open and made my way quickly to the foot of my stairs. Still half asleep, fear still gripping my chest, I slid the chain across on my front door and then collapsed onto the bottom step. The nightmare was fading now, but the emotions it had left behind were not abating. I buried my face in my hands and began to cry, long hard sobs that hurt my throat and chest.

I wanted free of this pain and would do anything to rid myself of it. I could not stand it any longer, I had never hurt this way before, never loved this way before, never felt such loss. For the first time I thought of suicide, it seemed a small price to pay for peace.

"When I see your face
There's not a thing I would change
'Cause you're amazing
Just the way you are"
Bruno Mars

On the 5th of May 1996 I met the most wonderful woman in the world. When I met her, she was in a bar with a friend and I was with a bunch of friends celebrating my birthday. Her friend disappeared with a guy from my party and the other girl got invited back to my student digs and the party resumed there. Once there we got talking and I apologised for being a little drunk.

She looked at me with big doe eyes and said, 'You won't be any use to me tonight then?'

OMG! I left people to enjoy the party and dragged the girl into my bedroom. What a wild night. The next morning, exhausted, I walked her home and was on cloud 9. I called her the next day under the pretence of seeing her again and, although I did want to, my main reason was to get her name – bad John.

Lizzie had the kindest heart any woman had ever owned, she had the patience of a saint. What started off as a one-night stand quickly developed into something more serious. She told me when the relationship seemed to be going somewhere, that she didn't want children…not at all…never. OK she didn't want children and I did, but I gave up my dream of becoming a father to be with her, I loved her, and that's what you do when you love someone right? Sacrifice.

She soon found out that I was, let's say, difficult to be with. I was an emotional guy with a victim complex in the way that I thought the world was working to make me unhappy. The littlest things could and did set me off, I got angry that I could not tie my tie for my graduation party, I would rage at not being able to put furniture together, even though I'd disregarded the instructions, I would scream, 'Why me?!!!' if it rained when I wanted to go out. I was stupid and dramatic, but Lizzie took it all in her stride and the longer we spent together the calmer I became.

She had a way about her, a stillness that I didn't think I would ever possess. She seemed to know me like no one had ever known me. Her understanding exceeded that of any other woman out there, I think that most of you ladies reading this would have walked without a glance back. I was not a bad person just a result of my upbringing, dominated by a mother who instilled the dramatic within me.

My mum was extreme in everything she did. She would get angry at the drop of a hat. My mother believed in telling you to do something once, if you did not do it immediately then she would hit out physically. I never knew that her voice had any other pitch than shouting. She would take me to the doctors for every little thing too, I walked funny, I sat too close to the TV, I was too thin. Only the walking funny turned out to be a 'thing'. The doctors told my mother when I was two years old that my walking on my toes was a bad habit. For the following thirteen years my mum would either tell me off or clip me across the head whenever she saw me walking on my toes. At the age of fifteen, after many visits to the doctors and the hospital, I was told that my Achilles tendons were too short and that I needed an operation...all those telling offs and hitting me had been for nothing, it wasn't my fault after all.

I had corrective surgery and had to learn to walk again with the help of leg callipers that I wore for six months. I had been bullied all the way through school and now the bullying intensified. Between my mother and the school bullies, I had no confidence, rock bottom self-esteem, had a victim mentality and an anger that could be all consuming.

Being with Lizzie was like a breath of life had been blown into me. She loved me so unconditionally, and it wasn't long until my confidence began to soar, my self-esteem was up and my anger was watered down dramatically. She was amazing.

Fifteen months after meeting we were married and for years it was everything I ever dreamed of. We would laugh and make love and we enjoyed life to the max. We never argued, well, very rarely, and even when we did it was over in no time. I couldn't stay angry at her.

My parents thought the world of her. They saw how happy she made me and always said that they thought of her as a daughter, not a daughter-in-law. Life was how it should be.

Our marriage was good, it was passionate and funny, and we loved each other with an intensity that is hard to explain. I have always been someone who loved to try new things, and not simple things either. I tried to make a cupcake business work, I had my own radio show, I tried my hand at band promotion, nothing worked, but it was fun and Lizzie was there every step of the way, being supportive.

I was romantic too. I'd try to make our anniversaries memorable. For one anniversary we sat on the edge of the Grand Canyon and watched the sunset, well, I did, Lizzie got cold and went to sit on the coach leaving me to watch the sunset alone.

We went to Egypt for another anniversary. I smuggled a letter to the pilot on our outgoing flight and as we came into land the pilot made an announcement:

'Ladies and gentlemen, can I have your attention please. I have a message for a Mrs Lizzie James from her husband, John. *Happy anniversary. I love you more with each passing year. I hope to spend many more wonderful years with you. I love you.* Let's all wish the happy couple a happy anniversary.'

All the passengers gave us a round of applause. I turned to Lizzie and she was crying with joy.

On the evening of our actual anniversary we were collected from out hotel room and led along the shores of the Nile. I had spoken to the manager of the hotel and arranged something special. We were led down to a jetty away from the rest of the complex and there we found it surrounded in lace curtains and in its centre was a candlelit table for two. We were served a three-course meal as we watched the sunset over the Nile, and no disappearing act by Lizzie this time. We clinked glasses and said, 'I love you.' We laughed at the waiter who would serve us our course and then run off to hide behind a bush to give us some privacy.

Being married to Lizzie was an honour.

"Staying with you

Gave us something to do"

Blue Oyster Cult

Ten years on.

Despite my sacrificing my dream of being a father I always had a niggle. Somewhere in the annals of my mind there was a resentment. I told Lizzie of my desire to be a father, we even made a compromise and had a dog, in fact, three dogs, as a kind of compensation. I treated my dogs like children, I bought them Christmas presents and called myself their dad, and at first it was good a solution, but longing to be a father haunted me, though I could not tell Lizzie for fear of making her angry or upset.

I don't know if she suspected my desire for children, but she started to change towards me. Lizzie started by being unenthusiastic about physical intimacy which was not great. Then she began to say no altogether. It was a task to even kiss her. Was this a fear that she would get pregnant? I don't know, but our sex life became non-existent. I tried a few times to sort the situation, I would ask her why she didn't want to be intimate and tried to explain that I loved her and wanted a physical relationship, but each time I approached the subject she would get upset and I would back off. After several attempts I stopped trying altogether. I felt unattractive, rejected. Yes, we still laughed together and enjoyed each other's company, but when the woman you love doesn't want to touch you it's a gut-wrenching feeling.

The years rolled by and we became more like friends than anything else. Sure, we had a good time when together, but the marriage began to mutate and then we began to sleep in separate bedrooms. Our rationale was that the bed was not big enough for the two of us and our ever growing canine children, but we both knew that it was an inevitable course of our estrangement.

I knew Lizzie still loved me, but that love had changed. I didn't feel desired anymore, it was as if I was invisible half the time, so I began to find ways to occupy myself. I began to go to concerts on my own, to hang out with friends more, I even went on holiday on my own. Lizzie did not even protest, she let me live a separate life. A part of me wanted her to object, to show me that she actually gave a shit, but nothing.

We drifted further and further apart, neither of us caring. The difference was that she was happy with how things were, and why not, she had a man who loved her, she went on holiday and spent the rest of the time watching TV or reading. She complained about me going out with friends, but when we went out together it was for a meal and then back home. It was frustrating for me living with my wife who was so distant, and the more frustrated I got, the more unhappy I became. The marriage dragged on for another seven or so years, why did I stay? Where was I to go? I was settled and had never been a *go get 'em* type of guy, not one to up and start again.

Then I got a new job in Hereford.

"Here in the valley of indecision

I don't know what to do

I feel you slipping away."

John Lennon

The job came out of nowhere. The care home I had been working in was close to my home in Worcester, it was perfect, but now, due to safeguarding issues, the company was given twenty-eight days to get out. The company left us all hanging out to dry, but there was one tiny light of hope. I was offered a job in Hereford for a month. I didn't want to. but it was work, so I thought, *'What the hell.'*

It was a long trek from Worcester to Hereford, a two-hour train journey every day that left me exhausted. Catch the 6am train, get to work by 8am, handle challenging behaviour for twelve hours and home at 11pm only to be on the 6am train the next morning.

Me and Lizzie had very little time for ourselves. My rota meant that I only had one weekend off in three, my other days off were week days and I spent those days lying on the sofa, tired to death. Lizzie would come in from work and see me there, no housework done, the dogs not walked and no meal cooked. In a way I couldn't blame her for feeling sour, I'd been at home all day after all, but the physical strain as well as the mental stress took every ounce of energy I had.

Our marriage was now stale, at least in my mind. I don't know how Lizzie felt because we didn't talk about much. Our conversations revolved around work, and even that transformed into a one-sided conversation – me, complaining about everything.

After a month I was taken into the office. I thought that I was going to be thanked for the work I'd done and wished all the best. Instead, I was offered a full-time job. At first I said no, I couldn't handle the travel, physically, mentally or indeed financially. The manager issued an offer – two days on, two days off and they would rent me a flat for in between shifts, PLUS, they would pay me the team leader wage I had been getting from my previous place. I accepted.

The work situation had improved somewhat with this offer, but I could not see a way for my marriage to get back on track. We had been sleeping apart for six or seven years and I had been feeling less than desirable for a mass majority of that.

We had our highs, however. In August 2014, we went to Rome to celebrate our 17th wedding anniversary. A tiny bit of me thought that maybe we could be romantic in the beautiful Italian city and maybe rekindle the love we had, but although we had a great time, it wasn't to be.

We left behind the sights of Rome and when I returned back home I threw myself into both work and play. I volunteered to work several shifts in a row, stopping at the flat in between shifts. I would stay away from home for a week at a time sometimes and it didn't seem to bother Lizzie at all. A part of me wanted her to protest, to tell me I should get a job closer to home, to say she missed me, but she never did.

Because I worked so much, my take home pay was excellent most months and on those good months, I would put money aside without telling Lizzie. This money financed my trips away to concerts and London West End theatres. I would tell her that I was staying with friends when actually, I was staying at a hotel. I would tell her that a ticket cost £60 when actually it was £140. I suspected that she knew what I was doing as her financial head was always screwed on. I had accused her of being money orientated more than once, but that came from her parents who had retired at fifty and moved to Spain on the money her father had saved, but even if she did know she said nothing and I didn't care.

I not only went to concerts, but also went to the States for two weeks on my own. I had asked Lizzie to come, but she'd said no, so I went on my own.

By 2015 I was working more than I was at home. I was now in the position of working five days a week but hating my job. Over the two years that I had been with the company there had been a few staff changes and with those changes came problems. It is my experience working in care that there is little actual *care* about, there is little support and a viciousness amongst staff against other staff. It was this hostility, that took the form of back stabbing, that was making me miserable.

Because of this all my conversations with Lizzie consisted of constant complaining and angry outbursts, not directed at Lizzie but at the soulless lot I had the misfortune of working with. I don't know what Lizzie thought of my constant and persistent ranting because she never said anything, she just listened.

Would it have been different if she had told me to shut the hell up moaning all the damn time? I don't know, but with this presented freedom, I took upon myself to rant more and more. I could come home for the weekend and still be complaining about the same thing on the Monday morning. Bitchin' was like an addiction and I was an all in junkie.

Then one morning I walked into work, my head still full of grievances from several days previous. I walked into the office and looked up at the staff allocations board and found which client I would be working with that day. As I read the board my eyes spotted a name I hadn't seen before.

'Hey,' I said flicking a nod towards the unfamiliar name. 'Who's Monica?'

"When I first saw you baby
You took my breath away
I knew your name was Trouble
But my heart got in the way"

Whitesnake

'Who's Monica?' I asked.

People looked at me with screwed up faces like they had just bitten into a lemon.

'Agency,' someone grumbled.

Agency staff have a terrible time in care, they are not considered a part of the team so they are outsiders, not to be trusted, not to be even liked. I, on the other hand, like agency, that is to say, I see no difference between them and the full time staff, I mean, how could an agency worker be worse than a lot of the people I was working with every day?

I ignored the snide looks and went to make myself a coffee before shift began.

I walked into the kitchen and across the other side of the range was a girl I'd never seen before. I looked at her and she looked at me and smiled. Now, when Hollywood do the "man meets woman" thing they have fireworks and hearts pumping and heads spinning…I 100% agree with that interpretation.

It was like my whole world exploded. I looked at her and drank in every detail; her raven hair, her deep brown eyes, her smooth skin, her smile that held a hint of nervousness. I thought I'd never speak again, how could I? What could I say to this woman? She was beautiful, so beautiful, and her smile...BOOM! OMG! I thought my heart would collapse in on itself as my insides twisted and my intestines spelled out *I LOVE YOU* in my gut.

'Hi,' I said approaching her, 'I'm John.'

She took my outreached hand which sent a shiver up my arm. 'I'm Monica,' she said.

'I know,' I said trying to be cool.

I don't know what happened after that, my memory is hazy because I was a mess inside. I'd never felt this way before, a feeling this damn powerful. It was more than attraction, more than desire, it was love at first sight – cliché, but true.

That day I watched her as often as I could, not in a creepy way, just that I couldn't take my eyes off her. Another thing I liked about her was that during our interactions that day she took the piss out of me. She was beautiful and fun.

But I was married and she was obviously out of my league. I had never, and still don't, have a high opinion of my attractiveness, I'm not down about it, it's just there, so to think that a woman like that would even look at me twice was just something I couldn't comprehend. I just enjoyed seeing her and being around her.

I discovered that she was thirty-five, thirteen years my junior; she was Romanian and had been living in the UK for less than a year. She had a boyfriend, which half stabbed my heart and half relieved it, and she had a son that lived with her mother back in Romania. She was also fluent in four languages, Romanian, English, Greek and Italian and could hold a conversation in several others. When she spoke, it was a sweet sound and there was a shyness about her that I found very cute.

I know, I know, you are probably reading this wanting to throw up at my gushing about this woman, but every word is true, what is the point of adding a literary flair when my real feelings will more than suffice.

I saw that other guys liked her too, younger guys, cooler I guess, nearer her age. Two guys in particular seemed particularly interested, but it wasn't love as I was feeling, it was lust, they both spoke about her as if she were a piece of meat sent to their workplace for their pleasure…it was disgusting and disgraceful, not to mention unprofessional.

Throughout the day I spoke to her as often as I could, just passing the time, asking if she was OK, asking how her day was going. By the end of the shift I had calmed myself and come back to reality that nothing can or will happen between us. She found me out as her shift finished to say goodbye. I smiled and told her that it was nice meeting her and she was gone.

Her leaving was like a kick to the gut and I laughed to myself at my stupidity, to think that a girl like that could ever be interested in a guy like me.

"My life has been such a whirlwind since I saw you
I've been running round in circles in my mind"

REO Speedwagon

I went back to Worcester, back to Lizzie, back to my three beautiful dogs. I tried to convince myself that I just had a crush on Monica, just lust maybe, like the other guys. Maybe the lack of physical intimacy was taking control of my mind, but I couldn't shake her picture in my head; I couldn't shake the feeling in my chest. This was awful and wonderful at the same time.

I'd never felt this way before. With Lizzie, it had been different, I'd grown to love her so much and that love had been intense and wonderful and sweet. However, the moment I had seen Monica it had been like a thunderbolt, an internal explosion...it had been instant.

The more I thought about her, the more I tried to fight the feelings I thought I had, the more I fought, the more I wanted to see her again.

When I returned to work I followed my normal routine and went into the office to see which client I had been assigned to. As I entered the office I was met by the team leader of the day.

'John,' she said without so much as a good morning, 'you're working with Monica today, okay?'

I swallowed as my brain scrambled to actually process what she had just told me.

'Yes, that's fine,' I heard myself answer.

I knew that my pairing with Monica was a punishment of sorts; *Put John with the agency girl, ha ha ha,* but I didn't see it as a punishment, I didn't attach any negative connotations to the pairing at all. I was delighted, excited, for the first time in a long time I looked forward to my day at work.

I began work at 7.30am, but Monica was not due to start until 9am, so I went about my day, supporting the client and being happy about it.

At 8.50am the front door opened and Monica entered the building. I was the first person she saw and the smile on her face was radiant, but my attention moved from her smile quickly to her scarfed head and then my own smile widened, like a stupid looking Cheshire Cat. Beneath her scarf she had dyed her hair and believe me it was not a good colour.

'Jesus,' I said laughing. 'What the hell have you done to your hair?'

Monica laughed. 'I knew you would take the piss,' she said.

'I'm not taking the piss,' I said, 'It's fucking orange.'

'It's not orange,' she said cracking up. 'Piss off.'

I burst out laughing. 'It's orange, I'm telling you.'

We really laughed, and in that moment my imagination went wild with *if we were together* scenarios.

'You're working with me today,' I told her.

She grinned a stunning grin. 'Good,' she said.

During our day together we talked about ourselves, getting to know each other. I told her that I was married but didn't really go into detail about the state of it, but besides, at this point I felt as if I would be married forever, as I saw no reason that for marriage to end. I spoke about my career in care, my several projects such as my radio show and cupcake business ventures. I spoke of my love for music (I was your typical rocker, with long hair passed my shoulders) and of the many concerts I'd been to. Monica listened with a constant smile on her face, she said that she would love to go to concerts and I invited her to go with me. We found out that we both had a love of Marvel movies and that Monica had a thing for Tom Cruise.

The most personal I got was talking about my school days and the bullying I suffered at the hands of the other kids.

Monica told me of her first day at work and of an employee who had told her to stay away from me as I was "no good". This slur had no factual basis but what it did do, Monica said, was raise her interest and, she said, she now realised that it was bullshit. I was happy, happier than she knew, that she thought I was a "good guy".

When Monica talked about her personal life I was surprised at how open she was – *very* open.

She told me that she had been brought up in Romania during the rule of Nicolae Ceauşescu who, though responsible for modernising Romania, enriched himself and ruled Romania with an iron fist. Monica had spent time on her Grandfather's farm until Ceauşescu's overthrow and death in 1989. She told me that her mother was abusive and her father too and that he was an alcoholic. She told me of her moving from country to country to find work so that she could send money home for her son.

My heart went out to the girl who had been through so much and come out the other side.

She did have a dark side, however. Monica spoke of her brother throwing her out not once but twice and, although the blame was squarely put on her brother's shoulders, she mentioned that she had lost her temper, smashing things in the house as well as screaming at him which had led to him throwing her out.

She told me about drunken nights and that she was taken into hospital where it had taken five doctors to hold her down because she was *going crazy*.

Monica delighted in telling me about her boyfriends too, and there had been a few. She had had an affair with a married man, she had had boyfriends in Italy and Greece where she had worked, some had been nice to her, some not so much. I asked about her son's father, but she told me that she had been seeing two guys at the same time so did not know who his father was.

All this very personal information was openly given to me and I listened not judging, more like enthralled, she had lived a colourful life, more colourful than most movies. But from all this, it was the love she had for her son that broke my heart. She had travelled the world to try and make a living to put him through school back in Romania and when she talked about him her eyes sparkled, and I fell in love with her more deeply.

"Something in the way she moves
Attracts me like no other lover
Something in the way she woos me"

The Beatles

My feelings for Monica had grown with each passing day, but also had my guilt. I was married and, although not perfect, I did love Lizzie and did not want to hurt her. I would lie awake at night, my Rottweiler and my Staffordshire Bull Terrier snoring on either side of me, my head spinning with indecision. On the one hand I wanted to tell Monica how I felt, but on the other hand I didn't want to upset Lizzie. There was also the fact that I didn't feel like Monica was interested. She had a boyfriend and, even though she had told me that she couldn't bear him, she was still with him and that had to be a factor.

Any which way, it was me who was hurt and I just had to find the path of least resistance. So, right or wrong, I decided to distance myself.

The next few times that I saw Monica at work I was not working with her and that was a relief. I began to speak to her less and less and when I did speak to her it was with an emotional distance.

'Morning, Johnny,' Monica said one morning.

'Don't call me Johnny,' I replied coldly, 'I fucking hate being called Johnny.'

With that she walked away and, although it hurt me to be like that, I thought it was the best course of action.

The next few times I saw her I was cold, icy cold. I tried to focus on Lizzie and my three furry babies and for a while it was working, but Monica was not letting go. She would squeeze past me at work even though there was room for her to pass comfortably. She would brush passed me, smile at me. She was not making things easy for me.

My mind was telling me that nothing could happen, my heart was telling me I wanted her, and my body? Well, every time she brushed passed me my flesh soaked up the feeling and fucked over my mind, giving my heart a deeper longing.

I thought being in love was relatively easy, you just let it happen and go with the flow, but fighting against it? Now that's a bitch. Fighting how you feel is like King Canute syndrome, it's impossible to hold back a tidal wave of emotion.

It didn't matter how much I ignored her, how I spoke harshly to her, Monica was still there smiling, and touching and being lovely.

I was standing alone in the hallway one early afternoon when I looked up to see Monica coming down the stairs. I wanted to leave but I couldn't. I could not turn away. I watched her, the way the sun came in from behind her lighting her up like some Heavenly creature, the way she moved, that glorious smile; the whole world seemed to stop except for her.

I realised that she was watching me, watch her. She stopped half way down the stairs and grinned at me. She looked down at herself and started to bob up and down.

'Look, they bounce,' she said, referring to her breasts.

I had been captivated so completely by the wholeness of her that I'd not noticed her body, but when she drew my attention, I watched her bounce and the wall that I had been building on my inside crumbled to dust. First, I had love to contend with, but now I had lust on top of that, and now I knew that I couldn't ignore this.

My biggest problem now, I thought, was how to approach it. I knew that she liked me, but not in a million years did I think that she liked me enough to go out with me. The other big decision I had to make was, did I like/love her enough to risk my marriage. If it only went as far as a confession to Monica then Lizzie did not need to know, if Monica did want to take it further then...oh, things were a mess – damn you heart!!

Then it happened. I was paired with Monica again for the first time in ages. I started my shift at 9am and Monica had been there from 7.30. I was told by the team leader that she was upstairs with the client. I nodded coolly, trying not to give away the joy and excitement that I felt. I ascended the stairs and saw her at the top of the them, yet was not greeted by a smile, but by tears. My heart sank.

'What's the matter?' I asked.

She shook her head. 'Nothing.'

'Obviously there is, what is it?' I asked again.

She told me that a co-worker had spoken to her harshly and that it had upset her. I knew the co-worker in question and harshly, was a very polite word for how she was known to speak to people. Her tone could cut concrete and her words could be vicious. I put my arm around her and told her it was going to be okay, that she was working with me and that we were going to have a good day.

'I didn't want you to see me like this,' she said.

Why? That was the question that immediately came to mind. If you don't care about me, why would you care how I saw you? Was my mind making this up or was there something there?

The rest of the day was spent amusing the client and talking again about our lives. Obviously, our professionalism meant that any personal details were said away from the client, like when he was in his room, but I relished these moments of alone time. Her candidness was astonishing, and if I thought I had gotten the 'juicy bits' of her life before, then I was very sorely mistaken.

Monica told me of her sex life and lack thereof. She told me that she rarely had sex with her present boyfriend as she didn't even like him, but she didn't know how to get out of the relationship. She told me again of past boyfriends, of a threesome that she'd had. She told me that she had worked in the adult entertainment industry. She had struggled, she told me, to support her son, and done everything to earn money. One such job was working as a Cam Girl under the name *Bad Gurl*, she would sit in a room in front of a web cam and men would pay to see her naked and touch herself. She said that she had enjoyed the work and even got friendly with one customer who would just pay to 'talk to her'. Rather than find this disgusting, I found it hot, but I am a guy I guess, and it was to help give her son a better life.

There were three things that surprised me about her confessions, however, one, it was the openness with no inhibitions; secondly, it was the matter-of-factness about what she said, *just here it is*, so what. Lastly, it was the paradox between what she had told me and the girl herself. She seemed so sweet and shy and…innocent.

My side of the conversation was based around my marriage. I told her of the lack of intimacy, of us sleeping separately, of my longing to have kids but never did. She responded with a mixture of shock and sympathy and a real understanding. I felt listened to for the first time in years, like someone was truly interested in me.

At one point in the day we found ourselves sitting alone and, I don't know how it came about, but we were holding hands, and not just holding hands, but Monica was massaging my hand – no, not massaging – touching? The way she slid her fingers over the palm of my hand was melting my internal organs. I was in love, I was aroused, I was…besotted.

I had to tell her how I felt, but how?

"Some people want to fill the world

With silly love songs

And what's wrong with that?

I'd like to know…"

Paul McCartney & Wings

A couple of days later me and Monica were paired together again. This was it, if it didn't happen today I might as well give up and just get back to my life. Our day's activities meant that we would be out of the house for hours. During those hours our conversation was casual at first, talking about anything and everything. A few hours passed by and Monica began to ask me about my marriage.

'How have you lasted in a marriage with no sex?' Monica asked.

I shrugged. 'I just have,' I said. 'My wife is amazing apart from that.'

'But it's not really a marriage is it?' She looked at me intently, expecting an answer.

'I guess we're more like friends than anything else,' I said.

I could not look at her, fearing that I would give away how I felt.

'I couldn't go with a married man,' she said, 'I know I've been with one before, but not again.' She looked at me. 'It's not right is it? Going with married people.'

I swallowed hard, it was now or never.

'I'll answer that,' I told her, 'but first I want to ask you something.'

'Do I like you?' She said immediately.

I was shocked. How the hell did she know that I wanted to ask that? 'Yes,' I said tentatively. 'Are you attracted to me?'

'Yes,' she said without hesitation, 'very much.'

'I'm attracted to you too,' I said.

I did not mention love or how strong my feelings were, this was good enough and reciprocated by the sound of it.

'Excellent,' I said, not knowing where to go from here.

I had been out of practice for so long I had no idea what to say or do, plus we were working.

We spent most of our time then just looking at one another, now and then we would touch each other's hand or arm, but even these small gestures were electrifying for me.

I could hardly contain myself, I wanted to wrap her in my arms and never let go. I had no idea why I felt so strongly, but there was something about her beyond physical attraction, something intoxicating.

Near the end of the shift I did the most unprofessional thing that I've ever done or would ever do again – I kissed her.

'John,' she said pushing me away, 'we're at work,'

I pulled myself together and walked away. I finished the rest of my shift without being so stupid again.

As my shift drew to a close I approached Monica when she was alone. My shift finished at 7.30pm and I was going to stay at the flat, Monica's shift finished at 10pm.

'Monica, do you want to come to the flat tonight?' I asked. I knew that her boyfriend was away in Bucharest.

'Yes,' she said. 'I'll come tonight, now go.'

I spent the next several hours like a cat on a hot tin roof I was so pumped. I took a shower and put on fresh clothes, I sat on the edge of the bed, my foot bouncing nervously. I looked at my watch every few seconds willing the time to fly by.

At 10pm I went to the corner to wait for her. I looked at my watch and saw time slip to 10.05pm…10.10pm…10.15pm. I text Monica and told her that I was waiting.

A few seconds later a text came back –

'John, I'm really sorry but I've got a lift home. I don't think us being together is a good idea sorry.'

"She says her love for me could never die
But that'd change
if she ever found out about you and I
Oh but her love is cold
Wouldn't hurt her if she didn't know…"

Bryan Adams

I hurt like I never thought I could. I had had no relationship with Monica, not even a discussion about feelings apart from *I'm attracted to you,* so why so much hurt. I thought that it was possible, after years of wanting validation that I was 'worthy', that this was another rejection, proof that I wasn't worthy at all. The night time brought anger, anger at myself for letting myself feel, for thinking that a girl like that could care for a guy like me. But in the cold light of day my mind was clear, and I knew that I could not let go of this – not yet.

I called Monica and invited her to Birmingham for a weekend. I told her that I knew she was nervous, but so was I. I told her that I just needed to see what would happen, how we would be together…she said *yes.*

I booked the hotel and told Lizzie that I was going to spend the weekend with my friend. This did not mean that I was cold hearted about cheating, okay, the deception was cold hearted, but the feeling of guilt was enormous, and on several occasions, I wanted to abandon the whole idea. Monica had her doubts too, and during the next couple of weeks she wavered between being excited and wanting to call the whole thing off. As the weekend drew closer I told Monica that I had paid for the hotel, which I hadn't, but by the time of the weekend I just wanted to be with her so much that I would do and say anything to make it happen. Even on the day of the trip I was to meet her on the train but had doubts she would be there – she was.

I found her and slid into the seat next to her. We kissed lightly and she looked at me with big brown eyes, a coy shyness about her. When I told her that she was beautiful she squirmed with embarrassment. I loved her timidity, it was so endearing.

When we arrived in Birmingham we headed straight for the hotel. Monica sat on a small bench while I checked in. I gave my name, but I was then asked my 'friends' name…I felt so stupid, of course I knew her name was Monica, but had never inquired as to her surname.

'Errr, Monica, Monica Jones,' I said unconvincingly.

The woman behind the desk looked across to Monica then back at me. 'Monica Jones? Okay.'

I could have died, god knows what she thought.

I took the key card quickly and me and Monica rode the lift to our floor. We looked at each other and smiled. I got the sense that she was as nervous as me, the shyness in her made me wonder how the weekend would go, but I thought that if we only lay and held each other, then that would be okay, I was just happy that I felt wanted again.

As we reached the door to our room I tried to act like the confident one. I slid the key card into the lock and swung the door open. I walked into the room with Monica close behind. I put down the bags and turned back to her.

'Well, we're here,' I said.

I was suddenly pushed in the chest. I stumbled backwards and sat down on the small sofa and at once she was on me. Her mouth was suddenly on mine, her tongue exploring my mouth, her hands tugging at her clothes and mine.

My mind was in shock, my heart beating like the feet of a speed induced tap dancer. Within seconds she was topless. She grabbed my hands planting them on her breasts. She felt warm and smooth. Then my brain clicked into gear and I began to kiss her in return and touch her, pulling off my shirt and pulling her close and tight.

She felt amazing, she smelled amazing, she *was* amazing.

She jumped off me. 'I'm taking a shower,' she said, 'come on.'

Jesus, what had happened to the woman that I had walked into the hotel with? The shyness had vanished in the blink of an eye and was replaced with a burning passion.

I lay on the sofa for a few seconds more before following her into the bathroom. My nervousness was through the roof, her behaviour had shocked me. I opened the door of the shower and looked at her. Sweet god she was stunning. Every inch of her was perfection. She was short in stature, about 5'2, but if I had believed in a creator I would have thanked him for his work here.

She pulled me into the shower with such force that our naked wet bodies slapped together and her mouth was on mine once more. Her hand slid between us, but her playfulness was doing nothing for me down there.

To be honest, the fact that she was the most beautiful thing I'd ever seen, coupled with her change in character, a character that was now fully in control, was extremely intimidating. I know in the movies that how Monica was being is every man's dream – and believe me it was mine too – but the movies will have you believe that you are as hard as a rock with excitement…nope.

'Fuck,' I said looking down at myself.

'Ssssh,' she said and kissed me again.

We showered and dried each other and then moved into the bedroom. She did everything to arouse me but the more she did, the more intimidated I felt. She was in total control and very focussed. My mind was all over the place and I felt so stressed thinking that she would never want to see me again, but all the time Monica was amazing.

'It's okay,' she said. 'What's the matter? Is it me? Did I do something wrong?'

'No,' I said, 'I think I'm just out of practice.' Was the only thing I thought to say.

'That's fine,' she said smiling up at me.

She lay her head on my shoulder. I pulled her close and I was in heaven. I was so in love with this woman, she was everything I had wanted, the complete package. She was stunningly beautiful, sexy as hell, but more importantly, she was kind, understanding and thoughtful.

When we weren't attempting to make love, we talked. Monica told me more about her time as a cam girl, she told me how she seduced clients and showed me how she could touch herself and con them into thinking she was masturbating when she was not.

I also took photos of her too, dozens of them, me playing the role of Alex Manfredini and Monica was my muse, sometimes coy, hiding her nakedness beneath the starched sheets of the hotel bed, sometimes without inhibitions going full *Hustler.*

That night we went to the cinema to see *Ant Man* and then returned to the hotel to try again. We made love, but it wasn't very good because of me, but again she was very supportive. We held each other again and she stroked my skin, I have a bit of a pot belly and she wobbled it and laughed.

'Don't do that, please,' I asked.

'Why?' she said stopping.

'Cause I'm fat,' I said.

Monica looked at me, a deep frown furrowing her brow. 'Don't be stupid,' she said wobbling my belly again, 'I love your body.'

I screwed up my face. 'I used to be really skinny,' I told her, 'but then I got older and got this,' I indicated my small pot belly. 'I've got a thing about being fat.'

She lay her head back down on my shoulder. 'I like it,' she said.

"When a man loves a woman
Can't keep his mind on nothing else
He'd change the world
for the good thing he's found"

Percy Sledge

The following day, we sat in *The Square Peg* in Birmingham having lunch. We talked more about ourselves, and Monica told me more about her parents. She told me that her father had been physically abusive to her and her mother, and that he had spent time in prison for not having a job, such was Ceauşescu's Romania. She told me that he had died on the street of alcoholism, of how, before he died, he had sold everything from under her and her mother leaving them desolate.

Monica said that her mother had also been abusive, emotionally rather than physically. She said that her mother had, on more than one occasion, told her that she didn't love her and that she wished she was dead. However, as she told me these things, there was little emotion in her words, everything was very matter-of-fact, very stoic. I got the feeling that she had built herself a wall to stop her from feeling anything about those times, and I didn't blame her; I thought my upbringing had been rough, but this was beyond rough, and all with a backdrop of poverty, of sharing a bedsit with her mother in a rundown apartment building with rats.

Then she told me something that was a little disturbing to me. Monica told me that she knew she would suffer the same fate as her dad, that she would die on the street, alone.

'Don't be daft,' I said. 'You have your whole life in front of you, you're totally different people.'

She shook her head. 'No,' she said, 'I know I'll die on the street. I don't mind, I want to.'

Such a declaration shocked me. Was she saying this for effect? And if so, to what end? She couldn't be looking for me to feel sorry for her, to win some emotion, she already knew how I felt about her, she *had* all of my emotions. I tried to placate her, but she wouldn't listen, she was insistent that she *wanted* to die the same way as her father.

Later, after a pleasant day, we sat in a café in the town centre discussing where we took things from here. I said that I didn't know how to tell Lizzie, but I'd have to figure it out as I wanted to be with her, Monica. Monica said that she wanted to be with me too, but she had no such confusion. She took out her phone and began to text.

'What are you doing?' I asked.

She was silent. She would wait for a reply and then text again.

'What are you doing?' I asked again.

'Texting Gabe,' she answered, her eyes fixed on the phone screen.

Gabe was her boyfriend.

'Why?' I asked.

'To tell him it's over,' she said. 'I'm telling him that I'll put his things outside the door and he can sleep in the lounge.'

I was confused. 'He's in Romania, right?'

'Yeah, so?'

'You're dumping him by text, really?'

'Yeah.'

'What's he saying?' I asked.

'Asking me why, and I've told him I've found someone else. He wants to talk when he gets back, but I've told him no, I've made up my mind.'

I laughed. 'Really?'

Monica spun her phone around, so I could read her screen. She was right, she had just dumped her boyfriend of five years via text while he was in another country. I didn't know whether to feel sorry for the guy or flattered by her commitment to me.

'Wow,' is all I could muster.

The next day we headed home, Monica to Hereford and me to Worcester. As I got off the train I felt a heavy heart, partly because I didn't want to leave Monica and partly because I had cheated on Lizzie, something I swore I'd never do. As the train departed I mouthed, 'I love you.'

Monica smiled that oh so beautiful smile. 'I love you,' she mouthed too.

Once again, my heart did somersaults in my chest. I couldn't believe this was happening, but even as I felt so elated, my stomach churned.

Now, how do I tell Lizzie?

"I heard the words come out
I felt that I would die
It hurt so much to hurt you"

Evanescence

I walked through the grounds next to Hereford Cathedral fear gripping my heart like a vice. My phone sat in my hand, Lizzie's number on the screen, my finger hovered over it too scared to descend and press it. What do I say? How do I say it? I felt physically sick. We were one month away from our 18th wedding anniversary. We had not discussed anything, no hint that this was coming. I could have thrown up and the guilt was giving me cramps.

I could put my phone back in my pocket right now and tell Monica that it had been great, but I couldn't leave Lizzie, yet my feelings for Monica were so strong and so real, and she had dumped her boyfriend to be with me, as unceremonious as that was.

I took a deep breath and called Lizzie. I closed my eyes as I waited for her to answer, somewhere inside of me I wanted her not to.

'Hi,' she said cheerfully.

Christ, this is awful, *I* am awful.

'Hi, you ok?'

'Yeh, you?'

'Errrr, I think we need to have a chat when I get back.' I said, my mouth dry.

'What do you mean?' She asked.

'I just think that we need to chat.'

'You're worrying me,' she said, I could hear a tremor in her voice. 'Tell me what this is about.'

'I'd just rather say it to your face,' I said.

'Say what?' she demanded in a voice tinged with fear. 'John, what's going on?'

For a few seconds I couldn't speak. I thought of making something up, of not going through with it. 'I've been thinking about us,' I continued. 'I'm not happy.'

Fuck, she was crying already. 'What do you mean?' she sobbed.

'It's like we're friends, Lizzie. Being in Hereford has given me time to think. I don't know if I can do it anymore.'

When she spoke now it was punctuated by sobs. 'I thought everything was alright,' she said.

'Yeah, but…I've tried to talk about things before. We are sleeping in separate rooms and we are not intimate and…'

'That's not everything,' she snapped.

'No, but I feel that I'm…I don't know.'

'Have you got someone else?' She asked.

'No,' I lied. I felt like Peter denying Christ, it hurt that much to say. 'Look,' I said, 'if we stayed together would we have a full marriage?'

Lizzie didn't even hesitate, 'No.'

I closed my eyes tight, that *no* was a dagger in my chest though I didn't know why. 'I'm all mixed up,' I said, 'can you give me 'til Christmas to sort my head out?' I don't know why I said that, maybe I was edging my bets in case me and Monica didn't work out, if so, then I was a real bastard.

'No,' she growled, 'I'm not fucking waiting five months to found out whether I have a marriage or not.'

'Then it's over,' I heard myself say. I think my brain must have said, *'Do it, get it over with.'*

Now it was full blown tears, a heart-breaking sound.

I told Lizzie that I loved her, that I would always love her. I told her that I wanted to tell her to her face, that I didn't want it this way.

'But,' I said, 'I guess this way you can't just leave.'

'Can't I?' She said. *Click* – she hung up!

"If a man is considered guilty
For what goes on in his mind
Then give me the electric chair
For all my future crimes"

Prince

This was the most painful time I had had so far in my life. I had hurt the woman I had married, the woman I had loved, the woman I *still* loved, and in doing so, had hurt myself. Like I said at the beginning, I'm not looking for sympathy, I had brought this pain on myself, but still, it hurt like hell.

To add to the pain was my own stupidity, in delivering the news and breaking up an eighteen-year marriage, I had neglected to think ahead, meaning that I had no place to go but back to Worcester and thus, face Lizzie head on.

Lizzie had every right to tell me to *fuck off.* She had every right not to let me near the house, but Lizzie being Lizzie she allowed me to come back. We met in town and had a pleasant meal, we didn't really talk about *us*, we talked about work and skipped around what was happening like jumping barrels in *Donkey Kong*. In my naiveté I thought things would be fine, but that changed once we got home, then the tears came thick and fast.

I stumbled through several attempts to make things better, but everything that came out of my mouth was wrong, a mish mash of apology and explanation. I told her again that I still loved her and that I always would; I told her that I never wanted to lose her, that I always wanted her in my life. I spoke the truth, but it just sounded desperate.

Lizzie was angry and rightly so, she was hurt and pissed off and I guess frightened, after all, she had made me her world for nineteen years in all and she had no friends to turn to. She had work colleagues, but none trustworthy. She had lost touch with her only school friend soon after we got married, and now she had no one.

'You wasted nineteen years of my life,' she spat.

'How is it a waste?' I asked. 'We had good times.'

'And for what? For you to just fuck off. Are you seeing someone else? Tell me.'

My first instinct was to tell her the truth and to just get it out there, but I looked at her red face, her cheeks burning with tears, the anger, the disappointment and the hurt, so much hurt.

'No,' I said at last.

'You said you'd never leave,' she said. 'You told me that even if you didn't love me anymore that you still wouldn't leave because you'd never want to hurt me. It was lies, you fucking lied.'

I couldn't say a thing. She was right, I had said those exact words and now I was, in fact, a liar.

It was some of the most uncomfortable days I'd ever had, the animosity was thick in the air and I deserved every uncomfortable moment, but Lizzie didn't.

I returned to Hereford determined to get out of Worcester as soon as possible. In the meantime, Monica had had to face her now ex-boyfriend returning from Romania and had indeed made him move out of the room, but he had refused to move house.

The house that they lived in was a shared accommodation containing three couples, all Romanian. Monica and Gabe had been living there for the majority of their time since being in England. He had tried to change her mind, tried to win her back, but she was having none of it, she wanted me and that was it.

She told me this over a drink in a local pub and I relayed what had happened with Lizzie, only an edited version, leaving out the fact that I had told Lizzie that I still loved her. I explained my situation and that I needed to get out and that I wanted to move in with her. At first, she was hesitant, her ex was still there and she didn't want to cause any trouble. I was desperate, so I pushed it until she relented, and the next week I moved in.

That night we lay together wrapped in each other's arms telling each other *I love you*. Monica made a joke about her ex coming into the room at night and stabbing us to death, she even jammed a chair up against the door. We briefly talked about how it may be uncomfortable at first with him still being there, but that conversation was soon forgotten as she rolled on top of me and we made love. Monica was a noisy lover and she had no thoughts of her ex's feeling when she was crying out in the night in the throes of passion.

The next morning, we made love again and as I looked up at her, watching the way she moved, hearing her sigh and moan, seeing how beautiful she was, I couldn't imagine life being any better.

"Tonight, I wanna to lay it at your feet
'Cause girl I was made for you
Girl you were made for me"

Kiss

I had seen another side of Monica other than sweet and loving, and the *other* side was the side that intimidated me – that of the sexual animal. I had never been shy in bed myself, but I had been in the desert for some years and now I was faced with a vivacious younger woman with an appetite.

I could have carried on and hoped for the best, hope I'd get used to her lasciviousness, but I was too much of a coward to front it out.

Before I moved in with Monica I made an appointment with my doctor and sat through an embarrassing barrage of questions about my sexual proclivities. I sat with the doctor and created a whole life for myself, though it be a life of sexual inadequacy. In the end I must have sounded convincing enough because I earned the prize – Viagra.

Men take Viagra for a number of reasons some of which are serious erectile dysfunction, I was taking it for what? Vanity? Insecurity? Either way it was a stupid decision born from a desire to *keep up* with the woman I was in love with.

I did not discuss my decision with Monica, I believed that, if it worked, it would be good for both of us, for my confidence, for our life together…at least that was the rationale.

The following few weeks were some of the best times in my life. Me and Monica seemed like the perfect couple. We had fun when together and missed each other like crazy when we were apart. Our love making was like something out of a porn film, the Viagra was amazing. Monica liked to make love everywhere, so when everyone else was at work or otherwise out of the house we would make love on the sofa down stairs, in the kitchen, on the landing, even on the dining table. We made love in the shower, in front of a mirror, in every position and then some. She was noisy and passionate, sometimes sweet, sometimes aggressive. Everything she did was amazing, I was always light headed after we'd finished our love making sessions. Even when people were in the house she dragged me into the bathroom and we made love on top of the cabinet after I had swept the bottles and cans onto the floor like in the movies. She even dressed up in a St Trin-ians style outfit that pretty much drove me insane with the way she looked and acted. She was not afraid of anything.

I mention our love making because this was the only time she seemed **not** to be the Monica that I knew most of the time. The funny, shy Monica who told me that she got embarrassed by compliments and said that she only felt beautiful when with me, turned into someone else during sex, someone with no inhibitions, someone in complete control, a stranger for that period of time. This was *9½ Weeks* on steroids. I wasn't complaining, I loved every second, but still…she was different. During these times I was under her spell, she *owned* me, my body, my mind and my heart.

The only time that went less than perfect was when some guys from work saw us together, and, you know people, soon the work place was rife with rumour. Now, Monica had told me that some of the guys at work had been coming on to her, so much so that I had suggested that she go to the manager about sexual harassment, but Monica told me that she could handle it. So, to stop the rumours and to abate the sexual harassment I openly admitted that we were together. This turned out not to be a good idea.

The first result of this admission is that the manager stopped us from working together. The second thing that happened was that Monica got upset. She told me that she was a very private person, which was a curious thing to say after everything she had told me on our first time together. She also accused me of wanting to brag about her. I asked her what she meant by this and she told me that I was using her as a trophy, showing off to everyone that I was with her.

I said nothing to this apart from deny it, but I thought it seemed a little arrogant to think this. The bad feeling lasted a few days but slowly things returned to normal.

For years my self-confidence and self-esteem had eroded, I had felt unwanted by my own wife, but now Monica had restored my confidence and with it came a surge of happiness. I had never been so in love with anyone in my life and I'd never been so happy. She came to Stoke to meet my parents and won over my mother, which is nigh on impossible to do. We even went to Romania so that I could meet her family including her mother and her son.

Her son was a fine young man, a little shy at first, but I was impressed with how intelligent he was, and he had a good heart; a happy, positive lad although he lived in a bedsit with Monica's mother in a building that was dark and depressing.

Monica was embarrassed to take me there, but I wasn't one to judge, it was not their fault and they were great hosts. Monica's mother told Monica (in Romanian) that she liked me because I was clean. I sat and literally broke bread with them in a dinner of Romanian sausage and goat's cheese.

I also met her brother who told Monica that he wanted her to marry me as he wanted an English brother-in-law.

It was wonderful.

On our return from Romania we began to talk about having kids of our own, Monica was still young enough and I was excited at the prospect of at last being a father, we even picked out names, Tara

Katherine if it was a girl and Ethan if it was a boy. Life was amazing. All my dreams were coming true thanks to a chance meeting. I was so happy.

"Leave me alone

Just stop doggin' me around"

Michael Jackson

2012

19th May 2012 will live on in my memory as a great day in football. I was in a pub near to Stamford Bridge in London, my eyes fixed on the TV screen above me, the whole pub squeezed together holding a collective breath.

Didier Drogba stepped up to the penalty spot and placed the ball in front of him. As he approached the ball it was as if it were in slow motion and you could feel the very air grow more tense with every step. He struck the ball and as it slid into the back of the net the pub erupted.

Chelsea FC were Champions League winners. The air was filled with the deafening roar of a combination of relief and joy, strangers hugged each other, and tears flowed freely from unembarrassed eyes.

After the trophy had been given, I squeezed my way through the crowd and on to the street. I called Lizzie, she answered on the third ring.

'Happy?' she asked?

'You watched it?'

'Of course I watched it,' she said, 'I know how important this is to you. Besides, I wanted to know what kind of a mood you were going to be in when you got home.' She laughed. 'Babies,' she said talking to the dogs, 'daddy is going to be in a great mood tomorrow, yay.'

I laughed as a fresh fountain of happy tears sprung from my eyes. 'It…it was amazing,' I said.

'Good, I'm glad they won for you,' she said. 'Go enjoy yourself, love you.'

'I love you too,' I said. 'COME ON CHELSEA!!!'

2015

I grabbed a drink from the bar in the *Yates Wine Bar* in Hereford and settled myself into a seat with a perfect view of the screen and watched Chelsea run out onto the pitch.

My phone buzzed.

Come home, the message read.

It was from Monica. She had asked me not to go out and watch the game a couple of times before I had come out, but I had always used a Chelsea game as a little break from everything. When I was with Lizzie I would go to see Chelsea play at Stamford Bridge, away games and even in Europe, but 2011 my friend Gary, the guy I travelled to Stamford Bridge with went to bed and never woke up – he was 50. I went to two or three Chelsea games after he died, but it was never the same. So, I had stopped going to the games and chose to watch the games in the pub instead.

My phone buzzed again.

Come back home. I miss you.

I text her back that I had only just come out of the house and that I would return after the game, I even asked if she wanted to join me, even though I knew that she would talk all the way through the game as she did every time that we went to the cinema.

I don't want to watch football. Just come home, you know you want to.

I tried to ignore the text, but as I tried to concentrate on the game my phone kept buzzing.

Come home, I'm lonely.

I want you.

Are you ignoring me?

Fine, stay in the fucking pub.

I didn't know whether she was playing or really getting angry, but I just text, *'Babe, I'll be home straight after the game, I promise.'*

My phone went quiet. I didn't know whether to feel relieved or worried that there was going to be an argument waiting for me back home. Chelsea were winning 1-0 already, but my mind was too preoccupied to enjoy it.

I text her. *'Are you okay?'*

Nothing.

Nothing for a good ten minutes, then…

I'm touching myself. I need to be fucked.

I abandoned the game and went home.

"I don't wanna fight no more

This is time for letting go"

Tina Turner

I have said previously that I loved going to concerts, everything from Bob Dylan to Iron Maiden, Prince to Download Festival, but as well as music events I also loved theatre and comedy. The downside to these events is that, to grab yourself a decent ticket, one has to book well in advance, sometimes months, sometimes a year or more in advance. That being the case, when I started seeing Monica I already had a few things in the bag. One of these things was a ticket for comedian Jimmy Carr. I had wanted to see Jimmy Carr live for years, but I could never get a good ticket, now I had a 10th row ticket for his Wolverhampton gig and I was buzzing about it.

I had told Monica about it before we got together, and she had told me that she was jealous as she'd always wanted to go to comedy or a concert. So, I had gotten her a ticket for Whitesnake, which was in a few months' time.

Now we were together things had changed. The thought of me going away for the night did not go down well at all. Monica asked me several times leading up to the gig not to go. I told her that this was a pre-arranged trip and that I was going on my own. I laughed about her wanting me to stay finding it cute that she wanted to be with me. However, on the morning that I was to leave things were far from cute.

It started innocently enough, she asked me to stay, to be with her, and when I still wanted to go, she tried seduction.

'Why don't you stay here and fuck me?'

As tempting as that was I really wanted to see the show, but things began to get more serious.

'Stay,' she demanded. 'I need you here.'

'What do you need me for?' I asked.

'I just do.' There was no other explanation but that.

'Look,' I said calmly, 'I've been wanting to see Jimmy Carr for years. I'll be back tomorrow.' I leaned in to kiss her, but she pulled away.

'Selfish bastard,' she snapped. 'You don't give a fuck about me.'

'How am I selfish?' I asked. 'I've had this ticket from way before we met, you know this.'

Monica came close to me, so close I could feel her hot angry breath on my face. 'Go then,' she snarled.

'Go to your concert, you selfish bastard.' She turned and lay on the bed with her back to me.

I couldn't believe what I had just seen and heard. This was not like her. Maybe she was ill, maybe I should stay. My mind, however, told me otherwise, that, if I stayed, I would be setting a precedent that I would never be able to go to anything again.

I said her name a few times, tried to say something, anything, to make this right. My parents had always told me not to leave on an argument, but Monica was non-responsive.

After a few minutes I left feeling melancholy. I was going to a comedian that I had waited years to see, I should have been upbeat and excited, instead I had a sour taste left in my mouth by Monica's strange reaction.

I got onto the train heading for Wolverhampton when my phone buzzed. It was a message from Monica. I opened it hoping that it would be an apology or a 'have a nice time' message.

Selfish bastard, it read.

I ignored the content of her message and messaged her back that I loved her and that I would see her the following day. What I got was a stream of vicious messages.

'I needed you here and you left, fuck you.'

'You don't care about me. You're just a selfish bastard.'

'I don't know whether I want this if you're going to just abandon me'

I tried to placate her by telling her how much I cared about her, loved her, was crazy about her, all of which was true, but she wasn't having any of it.

Eventually, her texts stopped coming and she wouldn't answer any of mine. By the time I arrived in Wolverhampton I was a mass of anxieties. I didn't like to argue, in eighteen years of marriage me and Lizzie had argued maybe a half dozen times and never over something like this.

I booked into my hotel and then called Monica. She answered, but no matter how I tried to keep the conversation positive it became a shouting match. Her aggression was stunning. She threatened to leave me several times and each time she did I felt as if my heart had been ripped out. I was angry too, I struggled to stay composed, but it was hard. People in the street were looking now, looking at this red-faced guy speaking into his phone in a shouted whisper and then holding the phone away from his ear as the person on the other end screamed.

The time of the show came around quickly and I left the conversation on an angry note. I walked into the venue in a mess, and throughout the show I just kept going over and over what had been said. Needless to say, there was no way of enjoying the show.

On my return the next day I was greeted at the bedroom door with, 'Babbbyyyyyyy!'

I was then dragged to bed for a marathon love making session. I went along with the pleasantries so as not to cause another argument, but if her aim the previous day was to ruin the show and my night, she had achieved her goal.

"Take my hand
Take my whole life too
For I can't help
Falling in love with you"
Elvis Presley

In the months following the comedy gig argument things returned to *normal*. The love making remained amazing, but it was more than that, much more, I had fallen madly, truly, deeply in love with Monica and Monica, by the same token, was in love with me.

We talked about getting married and having a child all the time. We talked about what it would be like to be parents, of course Monica was already a parent, but our conversations were filled with excitement about our own child. I really wanted a girl and even when alone I fantasised about mine and Monica's daughter – Tara Katherine. I would dream of taking her to the park and to Disneyland, of her riding on my shoulders, of me taking her to school. Monica said that she didn't know if she could have children again as she had had half a dozen abortions over the years. She told me that she just did not want children with anyone after her son, so she had aborted them when she fell pregnant. She even told me that she had aborted twins when she had gotten pregnant with her ex, her last boyfriend and feared that this assault on her own body might have damaged her somehow. On hearing this I would hold her close and said, 'If we love each other enough it will happen.'

Monica was so into the idea of marrying me that she had an email address of MonicaJames. I was so hooked on being with Monica that I called us Jonica. I couldn't believe how lucky I was.

We would find little moments to be alone, moments devoid of sex; touching, loving moments where we just looked at each other or I would make her laugh until she literally peed herself.

One such moment I dressed in a nice shirt and Monica dressed in a blue flowered Japanese dress. Everyone was out of the house but we two. I made dinner and we sat listening to music. Monica played Tina Turner's *Simply The Best* and told me that every word was about me.

Later we put on some slow tunes and we danced together, holding each other close and whispering, 'I love you.'

'I can't wait to marry you,' she told me. 'I can't wait to have your child.'

She was excited at the prospect, as was I. It was magical, like a dream.

Day after day, week after week I fell down the rabbit hole, deeper and deeper in love. Monica said everything I wanted to hear, and every sweet word made me crazier about her. She would tell me how handsome I was, that I was a good man and how I was the only man she would ever need.

I think people were sick of me talking about her, especially the guys that had drooled over her at work. My friend, Wayne, couldn't believe how happy I was – I had never been so in love. I even managed to shut up that little voice in my head that asked, 'When will this all turn to shit?'

I became obsessed with making Monica smile, obsessed with making her laugh. I would leave notes on the bed for her to find when she came home from work, like lyrics from the Shinedown song *If You Only Knew* –

I'd sacrifice my beating heart
Before I lose you

I watched YouTube videos on how to make towel animals like you see in foreign hotels. Monica would come home to find a towel swan or towel pig on the bed, anything to make her smile even when I wasn't there.

One of my favourite times of the day was when we climbed into bed together and spoon. Sometimes I would hold her, sometimes she would hold me, I didn't mind which it was, I just adored being that close to her and I loved falling asleep to the sound of her breathing.

I awoke. The room was dark and the ominous sound of wind whistled round the windows. I realised that Monica was not asleep beside me and I thought that she may have been in the bathroom. I waited, listening to the wind, but after a few minutes I got out of bed and went to see where she could be.

As I stepped out onto the landing I could hear a low moan coming from downstairs. I went to investigate and before I had even reached the bottom of the stairs, I could see Monica in the kitchen lying on the cold tiled floor in the foetal position.

I rushed to her and asked what the matter was, concern in my every word. She gave no answer and flinched when I touched her.

'Monica, what's wrong?' I asked.

Monica still did not answer, just a low moan.

I ran upstairs to get a blanket to cover her, but when I returned she was gone. I looked out of the window and I could see her stumbling up the street in the middle of the road in her pyjamas. I grabbed her coat and ran after her.

'Monica,' I said putting the coat around her shoulders. 'What's wrong?'

'Pain,' she said.

'Come back to the house, people will think you're on drugs like this.'

Monica shrugged off my hand. 'You don't care,' she said, 'how can you say something like that, go away.'

'Tell me what's wrong?' I said again. 'I love you, I hate to see you like this.'

She groaned again and again.

'I'm taking you to A&E,' I said.

I wrapped my arm around her, my chest aching at the thought of Monica in pain.

When we got to the reception of A&E the assistant asked what was wrong.

Monica looked up. 'Toothache,' she said.

The nurse came a few minutes later and gave her two Paracetamol and told her to see a dentist.

She never did.

The pain was gone by the time we got home and, although she hardly spoke, she managed to remind me three times that I had said, 'They will think you're on drugs.'

"I see a bad moon a-rising
I see trouble on the way
I see earthquakes and lightnin'
I see bad times today"

Creedence Clearwater Revival

'Jesus, Monica.'

'Fuck sake, don't be such a baby.'

'How am I being a baby?'

'Grow a pair of balls, be a man.'

This was beginning to piss me off. Monica had begun, what she called, *playing.* Her playing consisted of pinching my skin and twisting it, or her other favourite, planting a solid blow to my chest with her fist.

'You're such a bitch,' she said.

'What would you say if I hurt *you* like this?' I asked her.

Monica shook her head, and without another word, she threw on her dressing gown and stormed out of the room. I went to the mirror and examined my chest, two small bruises were forming around my right nipple and, though that may not seem like a big deal, the consistency of the *playing* was.

The playing had begun a few weeks before but had increased in intensity and frequency. Each time it had happened I had complained and each time I had complained Monica had admonished me for it. I didn't know how to stop the problem, and that is exactly what it was – a problem. It was a woman who was supposed to love me purposely inflicting pain – a problem.

There were two clear perspectives here, my perspective, that my girlfriend was *choosing* to hurt me physically, and Monica's perspective, that of me being less that a man for not wanting to take it.

The most confusing thing is that this playing came out of nowhere, it didn't seem born out of anger or frustration, there was no noticeable cause, like an argument, that kickstarted this. It was just, well, cruel.

Many things had gone through my mind since it had begun, maybe it was the whole baby thing. Monica had not conceived and the chances that she would, seemed less likely in our minds. Maybe it was tiredness from work, maybe stress manifesting itself in over-zealous play. Maybe, just maybe, I was actually over-reacting.

Along with the playing was the name calling. When first meeting Monica I had told her that I had a thing about being fat, this had drawn the response that she loved my body, a comforting approach of a caring girlfriend. Now she called me *fatty* all the time and, like the playing, any complaint was met with hostility.

I examined the bruises on my chest again and sighed. I shook my head and went downstairs to try and offer an olive branch. Monica was in the kitchen with Gabe, her ex. She was laughing, cup of tea in hand. When I entered the kitchen, the laughing stopped, Monica rolled her eyes and buried her face in her mug.

I flipped on the kettle and acknowledged Gabe with a nod.

'You okay?' I asked Monica.

'Fine,' she said coldly.

I wanted to discuss what had happened, but not in front of Gabe, and even though it was obvious that we needed space, he stood where he was, either too ignorant of the cues in the air or not caring, I guessed the latter.

'Are you coming back upstairs?' I asked Monica.

'You go up if you want,' she said not looking at me. 'I'll be there when I'm ready.'

I didn't even wait for the kettle to boil I just left, Monica closing the kitchen door as I did so.

I waited in the room for half an hour or more, my insides burning with the build-up of stress. When she did return she did not even acknowledge me, she just began to get dressed.

'What are you doing?' I asked her.

'Jesus,' she said snatching up her top, 'you're fucking choking me.'

'I only asked what you were doing,' I noticed that my voice sounded childlike so I coughed and deepened my tone. 'I mean are you going somewhere?'

'Fuck sake,' she snapped. 'I'm going for a walk around town, happy?'

Not really, I thought. 'I'll come with you,' I said.

'No, I want to go on my own.'

I smiled, trying to lighten the mood. 'Come on,' I said in faux cheerfulness. 'We can grab a coffee or some lunch together, have a good afternoon.'

Monica stopped what she was doing and stared at me. The coldness that emanated from her look was horrible.

'I don't want a fucking coffee, I want to go out and be on my own, is that alright with you?'

I was shaking inside now, part of me wanted to shout at her, tell she was being a bitch, but the dominant part of me just wanted not to argue.

'You want me to make you dinner?' I asked eventually.

'I don't know when I'll be back,' she said.

'Okay,' I said in surrender. 'I'll wait for you to get back and we can eat together.'

'Whatever,' she said as she walked out of the door.

Four hours later Monica returned. I had spent those four hours pacing the room, anxiety sitting in my chest like a rock. I had tried to think of ways to make this right, I even thought of apologising, but I couldn't think for what.

Monica walked into the room and I asked if she'd had a good day out.

'Fine,' she answered monosyllabically.

'What do you want for dinner?'

'I've eaten,' she said still not looking at me.

We went the rest of the evening without hardly speaking a full sentence. I tried several times to engage in conversation, but each time I opened my mouth my brain came up with a blank. I had nothing to say, not that would dilute the treacle-like atmosphere anyway.

As I settled down in bed that night, my heart still heavy, Monica spoke.

'Hold me,' she said.

I wrapped my arms around her and pulled her close, but something at the back of my mind told me that this was for her, not for *us*.

"I got a black magic woman
Got me so blind I can't see
That she's a black magic woman
She's trying to make a devil out of me"

Santana

'My friend Andreea has been in touch and she wants to come to the UK to live, what do you think?'

I knew that Monica was asking for my reaction, daring me to say no. I guessed that she had already said yes.

'That's great,' I said smiling.

Monica frowned. 'You don't want her here do you?'

I inwardly sighed. 'I honestly don't mind,' I said. 'It would be good for you to have a friend here.'

'Okay,' she said, 'I'll tell her to come.'

Just a few weeks later I was picking Andreea up from the train station. I had met her when I visited Romania with Monica. To be honest, I didn't like her, and she didn't like me. She seemed like, what I've heard termed, as a leech. She seemed to like being with Monica as Monica attracted attention from men and she was included by association. She was also brash and arrogant and smoked like a chimney. I had imagined, however unlikable she was, that she might be good for Monica, but upon her arrival that optimism soon turned to dread.

She arrived with no money, no job and no place to live. Monica provided the roof over her head by saying that she could bed down in the living room of the house. Next, she provided her with money to get her started. It quickly became apparent that Andreea was spending the money on cigarettes which led to her either eating our food, or asking Monica for more money, which she promised to pay back when she got a job.

Problems began to arise after the first few days. The first problem was that she monopolised most of Monica's time. If I wanted to spend any time with Monica, she was there, but even if I hadn't had minded that, both Andreea and Monica refused to speak English most of the time, so I would sit like a gooseberry as they spoke Romanian to each other. My only real involvement was if I babbled incoherently as they spoke, taking the piss out of the fact that I couldn't understand, which, surprisingly, Monica found funny.

The second problem was the lack of privacy. Monica had told Andreea that she could use our room when we were at work without discussing it with me. I would arrive home after a morning shift to find Andreea asleep in our bed.

The third and final problem was that, although Monica smiled and laughed and chatted to Andreea, in private it was a different story. Monica would rant about Andreea being lazy and not having a job, she would complain that she was asking for money all the time and tell me that she wished she had never said that she could come to the UK. She complained about her smoking, her hygiene, and the fact that she went through our food like an army of ants.

So, on the one hand I was stuck in an unintelligible conversation or having my ear chewed off by constant complaining.

A couple of times I tried to tell Monica to stop giving her money to force her to get a job, but each time I did I would be accused of hating her friend, of not wanting her in the house. In the end I cottoned on to the fact that Andreea was immune from criticism from anyone else, but Monica herself could say what she wanted. This resulted in my silence on any matters concerning Andreea, I just became the dumb sounding board for complaint.

Monica would also use Andreea as a means of attack. If ever we argued, she would say, 'If you were good to me I wouldn't need her here.'

This hurt me deeply. I had tried so hard to make Monica happy, sure I made mistakes, a stupid joke here, a slam of the door there, but all in all I tried to please her. I found myself trying to find a new way to communicate, a way in which I could stay clear of triggers that would upset Monica, this meant having conversations sans criticism.

It wasn't always easy, as Monica expected a dialogue not passivity, and she would set traps for me along the way.

'Don't you think Andreea is taking advantage of me?'

That was a minefield of a question and you'd better be wearing heavy Kevlar when you stepped into it.

The *playing* had also continued which went hand in hand with arguments upon any complaint. If I **didn't** complain, she would now pat me patronisingly and say, 'Good boy.'

One morning she was being particularly *playful,* she punched me with her fist on the left side of my chest. The punch was so hard that my heart literally hurt.

'Fuck sake,' I said jumping out of bed.

'I'm getting tired of you,' she said. 'I thought you were supposed to be a man.'

My anger was up. 'I am a man,' I said raising my voice. My chest hurt like a son-of-a-bitch. 'But do you think men should be punched like that?'

'Pussy fucker,' she said. 'You're such a victim. Even when you were at school you got bullied, you told me that, who the fuck tells people that? No wonder everyone at work hates you.'

I didn't know where that had come from.

'You haven't worked there for months,' I said. 'How would you know what people think?'

She laughed a derisory laugh. 'They used to tell me all the time what a piece of shit you were, and they're right.'

'Who? Who told you that?'

'Everyone,' she said, laughing again. 'Nobody fucking likes you. I saw Jo the other day and she said no one liked you, they couldn't stand you.'

Jo was a girl I'd worked with for three years,

I don't know what hurt more, the thought of everybody hating me, or the fact that, if these things had been said, Monica hadn't defended me.

I tried to get back on topic. 'This fucking hitting and pinching has got to stop,' I said as firmly as I could.

'You are a fucking pussy!' she screamed, slamming her fists onto the bed.

'And you're a fucking nutter,' I said back.

Monica suddenly turned to me, and in all my life I had never seen so much hatred. Her pupils were so dilated that all I could see was black and for the first time I was actually fearful.

'I FUCKING HATE YOU!!' She screamed.

She swept all her make up off the dressing table and tore her hair dryer out of the wall throwing it across the room.

'I fucking hate you! I…hate…you.'

She took hold of the collar of the shirt she was wearing and ripped it. She began to claw at her own neck and chest, deep scratches were carved into her flesh, many breaking the skin.

I began to panic as she slapped herself about the face, blood soaking into her shirt and bra from the self-inflicted wounds. I was watching the woman I loved having an accelerated meltdown.

I ran to her. 'It's okay,' I said throwing my arms around her. 'I'm sorry, I'm sorry.' I didn't know what I was apologising for, but I just wanted to stop this craziness, it panicked me, scared me.

Monica fought against me at first but then buried her head in my shoulder. 'I hate you,' she whispered over and over.

'That's fine,' I said, 'as long as you're okay, that's fine.'

"They say I'm mental but I'm just confused
They say I'm mental but I've been abused"

The Eels

Since the day of Monica hurting herself things had been hot and cold in the extreme. The hot times were usually sexual. Her appetite in this department could be voracious, but seemed to be purely pleasure for her, whereas for me, these times were a way to be close to her.

The arguments were a regular thing now, the reason for which could be anything from a comment from me that she didn't like, to her looking for a fight because she was tired. I was not wholly innocent here, as I was highly stressed with the situation and could snap easily too, slam doors, and be jealous of the time she was spending with Andreea. I even packed my bags a few times, something inside urging me to leave. But whereas my moodiness was petulant, hers was cruel. She would pick at my weaknesses like a scab, whether it was calling me fat, questioning my manhood or saying, 'I'm glad I never had a baby with you.'

She knew that that comment in particular would cut so deep, and she seemed to take pleasure in wounding me in this way.

The other way she could get under my skin was through the silent treatment. She would tell me to leave her alone, that she wanted peace. She would spend hours with Andreea or spend time in Gabe's room when he was out, playing computer games by herself.

Andreea was now living in the room next to ours, after one of the other tenants had vacated it. Monica had been instrumental in getting rid of that tenant by logging a complaint with the landlady, saying that she was lazy and didn't look after the house. She even roped the other house mates in on the act to give her complaint more credence. Monica had also had several shouting matches with the girl and in the end, it became impossible for her to stay.

Because I wanted to limit the fallings out the best I could, I had stopped complaining about the *playing* which had now evolved to pinching, thumping, kicking me in bed and pinching my penis hard.

I kept hoping things would change. I loved her more than anything in the world and begged the universe to set us on the right path so that we could both be happy with each other. I thought having a friend there would be positive, but it had merely emboldened Monica to separate herself more from me.

Several times when we argued, Monica had questioned why she was with me and told me that other people had done the same. When I asked who these *other people* were, she would say that it didn't matter.

She did, however, tell me that one of her friends in Romania had said to her, 'Why are you with *him,* Monica? You're so pretty, you could do much better.'

As a result of this comment, Monica had removed all photos of me from her facebook and blocked all the photos I had tagged her in where she was with me.

On several occasions she stood in front of the mirror, either naked or in underwear, and look at herself, running her hands over her curves.

'I'm so pretty,' she said.

Then she would smile at herself and then turn a look on me that made me feel worthless.

Over time the stress intensified within me, my confidence and self-esteem plummeted. I was confused as to why Monica was like she was. The tiny voice at the back of my head questioned why I didn't just get out of there, but the dominant voice told me that things could change, that if only I could change the way I was, then things would improve.

I was in love, crazily in love with her. She was an addiction and the thought of losing her, the thought of her not loving me, was more than my mind could bear.

I wondered if marrying her and having a family would be the thing that our relationship needed to cement it. Sure, the baby seemed a distant dream now, but that didn't mean that it would never happen. We would still talk about the possibility now and then, so that meant that we both still wanted it, right?

The stress was also affecting work. I was cranky because of what was happening at home and suspicious of everyone I worked with. Monica had told me over and over that nobody liked me and, even though in the beginning I believed this to be an exaggeration, the words had infected my brain and left me believing that I was universally hated. This fed into the hands of the 'bad element' within the workplace. They reported me to the manager, interpreting my quiet demeanour as negativity in my job role and falsely reporting that my mood was affecting the clients.

I even took a sick day to be with Monica and try and recover from a fight that we'd had the night before. I had never skived from work before and had had a clean sickness record for eleven years, that's how stressed I was.

I had no one to talk to. I was too embarrassed to talk to friends, I could not trust work colleagues, my parents were bound to over react. I just needed someone I could open up to. I didn't need advice or even a discussion, just someone to talk to. In the end I turned to the only person I trusted unconditionally.

I met Lizzie in Birmingham on my day off and when Monica was at work. It was good to see her and there was no animosity between us, in fact, things were very pleasant.

We began with general conversation, starting slowly, both of us obviously nervous to be in each other's company again. We had spoken on the phone a few times in relation to the dogs and, when me and Monica made our dating official, I had enough respect for Lizzie to tell her.

Our conversation moved along and eventually evolved into me complaining about Monica and her behaviour. I told her about the hitting, the silent treatment and the fact that I spend my time either angry or walking on eggshells, tip toeing around her so as not to fight.

Lizzie listened without external judgment. Inside she was probably thinking, *this is karma*, but she never showed it if she was. She told me that I deserved better and that I had been an angry personality back in the day but had changed over time becoming calm and an easier going person and that, if Monica was making me angry, it was a step backwards. I listened as she talked, and my heart warmed to realise that she still cared that I was okay.

We had a nice lunch and spent a pleasant afternoon together. When we parted I watched her wave goodbye, tears were forming in her eyes and she turned away so I wouldn't see her crying. As she disappeared from view my heart grew heavy with regret and guilt – how could I had ever hurt such a wonderful woman like Lizzie.

"Countless sleepless nights

Never ending fights

I'm trying to make your dreams come true"

Lenny Kravitz

How did I fix this?

I could walk away, but where would I go? I could stay and put up with what was going on or…or what? I guess I could kill her.

I may have laughed at the latter option, but a morning, a week previous, she had woke me up at 4.30am by banging about the bedroom getting ready for work, not caring about anyone but herself.

I had buried my face in the pillow and mumbled something like, 'Jesus, I've got to go to work later, I'm going to be shattered.'

This had caused Monica to fly into a rage which had consisted of a golden oldie collection of insults including questioning my manhood, calling me a piece of shit and the new one, calling me a spoiled brat. I very much doubted, by the use of the phrase in its attributed context, that she actually knew the meaning of *spoiled brat.*

Needless to say, after she had stormed out I was left with a feeling of anger and regret for complaining in the first place.

I watched her leave for work on her push bike from the bedroom window and, to my shame, I wished for a fatal accident. Does that make me a bad person? I can't answer that, I only know that I hated being with Monica when she was being a bitch, but for some reason I could not bear the thought of living my life without her.

I knew that Lizzie was right, I didn't deserve being treated the way that I was, but I was at a loss as to how to fix it. With Lizzie, all problems were discussed, but with Monica that was a treacherous thing to do, but what were my realistic options?

I paced the room for an hour before she came home from work. A shot of panic ran through me when I heard her come in through the front door, several minutes later she came into our room, a smile spreading across her face when she saw me.

'Hi, Baby,' she said gently kissing me. 'I'm so tired.' Then, 'Guess who I saw today? Jo. I haven't seen her in ages.'

'You saw her a few weeks ago,' I said remembering the conversation in which Jo had told her that everyone *hated me.*

Monica looked at me. The smile was gone. 'I haven't seen her in a long time,' she reiterated.

'But, you said...' I stopped. This was a rabbit hole I didn't want to go down.

'What?' She asked. 'Are you calling me a liar? I can't handle an argument tonight, I just want peace. Please give me some peace.' She grabbed a towel and headed for the bathroom.

I sat on the edge of the bed, my hands shaking. She had said that she'd seen Jo a few weeks ago, I was sure of it. Was she lying? Had I been mistaken? This wasn't the first time I thought she had said something, only for her to contradict it at a later stage. I felt as if I were going mad. I didn't know whether what I was hearing was actual reality, or all in my head.

When she returned, I said nothing more. I tried to smile and have a good evening, but Monica was mad now and spent the rest of the evening talking to Andreea in Romanian.

When we eventually went to bed Monica asked me to hold her, and like an obedient pup I did. I fell asleep with no discussion about the way I was feeling, but I told myself that I would try and give Monica what she desired – peace.

Starting the next morning I made a conscious effort to go on an all-out 'charm offensive'. I cooked for her, I held her at night when she wanted me to, I made love when she wanted to, I stroked her back until she fell asleep; I cooked for her, I made her laugh, I told her she was beautiful, I went shopping with her and helped her pick out clothes, I did everything I could to please her. Monica responded well to my efforts, we even went out together, just us two. We ate and laughed, and Monica drank her usual Jack Daniels and Coke, I felt she was once again the Monica I had fallen in love with.

I must admit, however, that a small part of me feared a relapse. Because of this, I clung desperately to the *light* and struggled to hold off the *darkness*, I knew that one word out of place, one foot wrong, could spark the devil in Monica and we would be back to square one.

I monitored every word, even my thoughts, I controlled anything that could be perceived as a negative action. I ignored or laughed off the pinching and the thumping. I would listen to her complain about Andreea or explain to me how the girls she worked with were terrible carers compared to herself.

I got to be really good at judging her mood just by her expression. Sometimes I would get it wrong or make a bad joke maybe, and then the expression would change, I would then have to try and pull it back before she got mad, either by trying to laugh my way out of trouble or a speedy apology.

Peace had to be kept.

But it was tiring, physically, psychologically, but especially emotionally, and little by little the blanket of peace that I had so carefully woven began to fray.

In desperation I turned to her friend, Andreea.

"And I meant every word I said

When I said that I loved

I meant that I loved you forever"

REO Speedwagon

Monica and I had had a fantastic few weeks, so much so, that the anxiety that had become so ingrained in my emotional make-up was abating. I was smiling most days and truly enjoying life. We had even started trying for a baby again and talking about marriage, as soon I got my divorce from Lizzie.

Monica had a shining light about her again, she was an angel and being with her was heaven. I longed for her to return from work just to see her. She was spending less time with Andreea now, which made me happy too.

We would spend time watching movies and laughing, going to the cinema and of course, making love.

I couldn't envision a life without Monica and the way I felt was the way I imagined addicts felt about their drug of choice – Monica was my habit and I loved being high.

Even the *playing* had stopped. The insults were replaced by things such as, 'You're the only one I ever want to be with,' and, 'my only dream is to have a family with you.' She even talked about me becoming her son's step-father.

So, I was all the more shocked at the coldness she displayed as I walked into the kitchen. Monica pulled away from me as I came up behind her and put my arms around her waist.

'What's the matter?' I asked.

'Nothing,' she said flatly.

'Is it the time of the month?' I joked.

'Just leave me alone.'

'Sorry?'

'Just leave me alone,' she said without looking at me.

I was taken aback. I had done nothing wrong and, once again, this ice-cold front had come out of nowhere. It wasn't fair. I didn't deserve to be treated like this, or at least I deserved an explanation as to why I was being treated this way.

I could have walked away, I could have given her space, but damn it, why should I continue to go through this time and time again.

'Why do you have to be like this?' I asked.

'Like what?' She said and then, 'Oh, go away.'

'No,' I said, standing my ground. 'I come in here and give you a hug and you're being a bitch.'

'Fuck off!' She screamed. 'I can't stand you near me.'

'What the hell have I done to deserve this?'

She looked at me and shivered dramatically, a look of disgust on her face. 'I can't stand you touching me. I just want you to stay away. When you touch me I feel sick.'

I can't explain how much that hurt and how angry that made me feel. She knew just what to say to cause the maximum emotional damage.

'Just stay away from me,' she said again.

'I'm fucking sick of this,' I said.

'I'm sick of you,' she retorted. 'I wish I never met you.'

'You want to sort yourself out,' I said, my voice shaking. 'There's something wrong with you.'

'Leave me alone, leave me alone!' With that, she slapped herself in the face. 'You're making me crazy,' she said. 'You're driving me mad.'

'What are you doing?' I asked, concerned.

'You don't care about me,' she said. 'You just want a pretty girl to show off with.'

'You think too highly of yourself,' I said.

Monica began to cry and dropped to her knees starting to shake. I watched in shock as she clung to herself and she rocked back and forth.

'Monica, come on,' I said, crouching beside her. 'Come on. It's going to be okay.'

She pushed me away and leapt to her feet. Before I knew it she grabbed a knife and ran into the downstairs toilet. I took after her and tried the door, but she had locked it.

'I want to die,' she screamed.

Silence.

I called her name several times but there was no answer.

One of the girls who lived in the house came running downstairs and asked what the matter was.

I told her what had happened and she too knocked on the door.

'Monica,' she said. 'Monica, just tell me if you're okay.'

Silence.

I was just about to kick in the door when it opened and Monica fell into the hallway as if she was going to faint.

'I want to die,' she said again.

'Let me see this,' I said, taking her arms and looking at them.

Running off with the knife and not answering when I called her name was supposed to have made me believe that she had committed suicide, or at least badly hurt herself, and yes, she had used the knife on her wrists, but the marks were that of the lightest of scratches.

Now it was my turn to be dramatic. Instead of calling her out on her silliness and to prevent anymore arguing, I acted as if it had been a real attempt to take her own life.

'Monica, I love you,' I said forcing sadness into my voice. 'I don't want you to die. Come on, sweetheart, let's go upstairs, you need to lie down.'

Reassuring the girl that I would take care of Monica, I led her upstairs and put her to bed.

I left her to sleep and came downstairs. I stood in the kitchen trying to calm myself when Andreea came down and took herself outside for a cigarette.

I joined Andreea and asked if I could talk about Monica. I told her of the problems I'd been having, of the explosive temper, the pinching and the hitting – *the playing.*

'Slap her,' she told me.

I was a little surprised. 'I'm sorry?'

'Slap her,' she repeated matter-of-factly.

'I'm not slapping her,' I said frustrated.

'Up to you.'

'I'm not slapping her,' I said again. 'There's no way I'm hitting a woman.'

'Look, John,' she said. 'You are looking at this from an Englishman's point of view, but Monica is Romanian. You need to act like a Romanian man. Romanian men are *men* and they are tough.'

'I don't think it's tough to hit a woman,' I told her.

'You have to be like a Romanian man,' she said. 'If you slap her then you'll show that you're not taking shit. You will show her who is boss, and everything will be better. She will have respect for you.'

For the next few days I pondered what Andreea had said. It seemed stupid, but Andreea did know the Romanian culture and maybe Monica was pushing me to be more like the guys in her country, maybe that's what all the *questioning my manhood* was about.

I didn't like the idea of hitting a woman, of hitting anyone, but I was at the end of my rope, so to speak, and desperate times called for desperate measures.

Time to be a Romanian man.

"You started something
That you just couldn't stop
You turned the ones that you love
Into the angriest mob"

Shinedown

Yet again, things went smoothly, but this time I did not, could not, relax. My anxiety levels were constantly high, my suspicions of something going wrong meant that I feared seeing her, as the uncertainty of which Monica I would get, was enough to give me a headache.

But I still could not bear the thought of leaving her. Why couldn't I even contemplate that? Seriously? What was it that kept me with this woman, kept me *willing* to be subjected to the continuous cruelty whether it be physical, verbal, psychological or emotional.

Throughout my life I had never been a stranger to cruelty. My school days were filled with bullies and beautiful girls who would tease me and then unleash a vicious comment about my appearance. I was hit, spat at, tied to a fence with wire and left for the whole school to laugh at.

Why was I bullied? Because I was 4'11 and as thin as a rake. I also wore glasses before icons like Harry Potter made them trendy. Also, as I told you earlier, I also had a walking disability that led to me wearing leg callipers – I was a speech impediment short of a full set.

But yes, I was bullied; many people were and still are, but as cruel as it was, I convinced myself it was a part of school life.

When I left school and started to work for a living, I discovered that cruelty didn't end when you left school. My first job was on a brick factory where my dad was the night watchman and kiln fireman. My dad was an easy-going guy who liked to do his job and support his family. My dad was also the friendliest guy you would ever hope to meet, he wouldn't have cared if you were a homeless person or the Queen of England, he treated everyone the same and was friendly with everyone, unfortunately, this meant managers too. The other workers saw him as a *suck up* and because they were too cowardly to pick on my dad directly, they chose to turn their attention to me. Don't get me wrong, I'm not blaming the bullying at work on my dad, I'm blaming it on the tiny brains of my co-workers who would verbally abuse me and threaten me on a daily basis.

My experiences did benefit me in the way that I toughened up and soon, I was the man with the mouth and could cut a bully to pieces with a sentence. I remember a guy threatening me at work in front of a crowd of people, his chest puffed out, his bravado on full display.

'Who are you staring at?' He said, standing as tall as he could.

I looked him up and down. 'Not sure,' I said casually.

'You trying to be funny,' he said rhetorically. 'I'll fucking hurt you.'

Everyone looked at me, waiting for my fear filled response.

I waited a few seconds and then looked at him surprised. 'Sorry, is this the part when I'm scared?' I asked.

I could see a tiny waver in his toughness as a few people sniggered.

The bully's shoulders went back and if he were a peacock, I'm sure he would have fanned out his tail feathers aggressively.

'I'll take you outside and kick your fucking teeth in,' he said posturing.

I looked at him confused and then put on a childlike voice. 'I'll kick your teeth in,' I mimicked. 'Fuck man, what are you, ten? People used to say that at school, you want some new material.'

The gathered crowd started to laugh, and the bully started to shrink.

'I'll have you outside,' he said, before walking away.

He never did.

My life became bully free for some years, but, I must admit, the dark side to my new confidence is that my mouth would get me into trouble. I lost several jobs because I couldn't keep my mouth shut, I lost friends because I couldn't shut up, I even got banned from being a student representative at college because I couldn't shut my trap.

But at least I wasn't being bullied, right? Not until university anyway, when I found myself in a relationship with Vicky.

Vicky was beautiful, funny, smart and violent. Her idea of fun was to scar the backs of my hands with scratches. She was, like Monica, very sexual but a total fucking psycho. The relationship lasted seven months and, although she screwed with my head I had friends around me to turn to.

It took me the summer to get over it.

Fast forward to 2016 and the stress of my present situation was affecting all aspects of my life including my work. I was now a regular in the office being questioned about my conduct which consisted of being withdrawn and not engaging with staff. I know, I was in care so what did these complaints matter as long as I cared for the clients? A lot, apparently. The managers took every complaint seriously whether it related to the job at hand or not, that was just how the management rolled.

Unfortunately, I was unwilling to talk to my colleagues about what was going on because I believed all of them to be untrustworthy after Monica's many comments about me being hated. On the other hand, the staff were more than willing to put in a complaint than ask myself if something was wrong.

It was getting hard to hold myself together. I found that the stress was making me agitated and that agitation resulted in a change in my tone of voice, a tone of voice that didn't suit Monica, I would slam doors and walk out of the house without telling her where I was going; result? More arguments.

As time went on I knew that our confrontations would come to a head, I could feel it in the air between us. Something was coming, and, as we moved into the late afternoon of what had been a pleasant enough Sunday, I knew it would be that evening.

"I'm gonna knock you out
Mama said knock you out"

LL Cool J

'I fucking hate you! Piece of shit! I wish I never met you, you've ruined my life.'

'How have I ruined your life?'

'You just have. I can't stand you. I can't bear to even look at you.'

'Who do you want to look at? Baldy bastard?'

I couldn't help that. There was a guy who lived in the house we were in, his girlfriend had left him because he was hitting her and since then he had taken a shine to Monica. Monica being Monica, had giggled her way through many a conversation knowing, I suspected, that it was making me jealous. Monica liked attention despite her insistence to the contrary.

'You're sick,' she said. 'You're fucking mental.'

'I'm mental?' I said. 'I don't even know how this fucking argument started. I *was* having a good day.'

'You fucking started it,' she screamed at me, 'by being a spoiled brat.'

'Do you know what that means?' I asked in all seriousness.

'Yes,' she said. 'You.'

I was shaking with stress and my stomach was turning repeatedly. I truly did not know how this had all begun. I thought back over the last hour and saw, in my mind's eye, the downward trajectory of Monica's mood, but I could not pin point any origin.

'Just leave me alone,' she said. 'I don't want to talk to you today. I don't want to look at you.'

Monica was dressing and as she pulled off her top to put on her bra she turned her back. This had become a *thing*. If she was mad and she had to change she would turn away or even ask me to step out of the room. It was a distancing technique I knew, but damn it, it still hurt.

'I'm going out,' she said, 'and before you say anything, no, I don't want you to come.'

'We can't keep doing this, Babe,' I said.

'Don't call me babe,' she demanded.

'Babe…babe…babe,' I said childishly.

'You're so fucking stupid,' she snarled.

'Sorry,' I said quietly. 'I love you so much and we keep doing this shit all the time. I just want a happy life with you.'

'Then behave,' she said angrily. 'You are the luckiest man there is. You get to come home every night and have a beautiful woman in bed with you. And then you act like a bitch.'

She looked in the mirror and smiled at her own reflection. She looked back at me sans smile.

'I'm going out. You better give me peace when I get back.'

Monica walked out leaving me to collapse on the bed in pure frustration, the morning running like a film on loop in my head trying to see what I had done wrong and what I could do to fix it.

I felt as if I could never do right, that no matter what I did or said it would always be counter to what she wanted me to do or say. I tried backing off if she started getting mad, I tried being extra nice, I even tried fighting with her hoping that that would release tension.

I was always wrong.

I began to question the type of person I was. I saw the way she interacted with the other guys in the house, including her ex, and it was so different to how she responded to me. I wondered what I could do to have the Monica that they seemed to be having.

I decided to give her some space. Maybe by giving her exactly what she wanted she would react more favourably.

I spent the whole day trying to watch movies, but nothing could hold my attention. I wanted to go for a walk into town, but I knew if I saw Monica I would be accused of stalking her or something.

She came back home late. I did not ask where she'd been or question her in any way, even though I wanted to. Instead, I offered to make her a meal. What I got in reply was an icy glare and three words:

'Leave me alone.'

The house was quiet, the rest of the house were working the night shift so me and Monica were by ourselves. I waited in the room for several hours as Monica sat downstairs giving me the silent treatment again.

As the night drew on, being ignored began to get under my skin. I began to get antsy and I knew that my nerve was going to break.

When it did, I could not stop myself from wanting to make things right. I went downstairs and what I saw alarmed me.

Monica was sitting at the dining room table, earphones in listening to music, a litre bottle of Jack Daniels in front of her. I had flashbacks of what she had told me about her father being an alcoholic. I remembered what she had told me about her prediction for herself, that she would die on the street, that she would be like her father. I remembered the story of five hospital staff holding her down as she fought them in a drunken fit of rage.

I did not want that for *my* Monica.

I tried talking to her at first, but she ignored me. I took an earpiece out of her ear only to be pushed away without a word and the earbud replaced.

My next move was stupid, but I did it out of concern and pure panic. I grabbed the bottle of Jack and took it into the kitchen and, without even thinking, I poured it down the sink.

When I came into the lounge she asked me where her drink was and I told her what I had done.

Monica was enraged. In one lightening move she punched me full in the face.

The words of Andreea shot into my head: *'Slap her…you need to be like a Romanian man.'*

I slapped her across the face.

Rather than her show me respect for standing up to her she punched me again and again then, coming up close to me, she spat in my face.

'CUNT!' She shouted.

As I recoiled she attacked me in earnest. Throwing solid punches into my face and body. She kicked me over and over in my hip and thigh, all the time screaming abuse, most of which was incoherent.

I could do little but raise my arms to protect myself, I had never before received such a sustained attack, and this from a woman who was supposed to love me.

'Monica. Calm down,' I repeated over and over.

I tried to hold her, to dampen the rage, but she kicked me in the balls and I was forced to let go.

When she hit me, it was with her fist, no slapping here. And she was strong. She was little over five feet tall and slim, but Christ she could throw a punch.

I don't know how long the attack lasted, but it seemed to go on and on and on. When it subsided it was because she was exhausted.

I backed away, relieved she had stopped, and went upstairs. When I came back down I had a packed bag in my hand and I headed for the door.

Before I could open it Monica threw herself between me and the exit.

'Where are you going?' She asked, not one sign of an aggressive tone was in her voice.

'I can't take this, Monica,' I said. 'I can't be hit like that.'

My brain was scrambling to think of the next train to Stoke to go to my parents.

'Don't be silly,' she said sweetly. 'Let's go upstairs. Come on. I'm sorry.'

I looked at her. Her face was so sweet, her eyes full of apology.

She touched my arm.

'Monica,' I said softly, 'I love you, but I can't do this.'

I could already feel my insides collapsing, my heart swelling. She looked so beautiful, so…innocent.

'Come on. Put your bag away and don't be silly,' she said coming closer to me.

'That was bad, Monica,' I said, but I had already lost.

Monica smiled and stepped closer still. 'Let's go to bed,' she said. 'Come on,' she said, taking my hand. 'I love you.'

She led me to bed.

"The faster we're falling

We're stopping and stalling

We're running in circles again"

Sum 41

The morning after the big fight I found it difficult to move. My years of working in care had given me sciatica but for years I had had it under control. However, the constant barrage of kicks to my hip from Monica had flared it up again and the pain was excruciating.

On my way to work I got a text message from Monica. *'Hey, Baby, how are you?'*

Maybe I should have kept my mouth shut, maybe I should have just answered, *'I'm fine. I love you.'*

If I had answered that, given her what she was looking for, then I may have been okay, at least as far as another fight went.

'My back and thigh are killing me,' I text.

'Why, Baby?'

'Because of you kicking me last night.'

My stupidity at this reply is unforgivable. I knew as I wrote it that I was once again stepping into the scorpion's den, but that didn't make it any less true.

'I can't fucking believe you,' she wrote. *'You dare fucking blame me for that? Fuck off.'*

My attempts at retraction were met with silence, so I settled into the thought of yet another sentence of being sent to Coventry when I got home.

The last several hundred yards to work were uphill and it took its toll on my back and hip. By the time I reached the front door of the care home I could not feel my legs. I opened the front door and fell to the floor.

'Hello, somebody,' I called.

'Hi, morning,' someone answered. No one came.

'Help me,' I called being more explicit.

Despite the unfriendliness of most of the staff I worked with when they saw me lying on the floor, my face set in a grimace of pain, they did spring into action. Someone got me a pillow, another person called an ambulance. Within fifteen minutes the ambulance was there. I was put on a stretcher and given gas and air and rushed off to hospital. Every time I stopped breathing the *laughing gas* the pain would hit me like a tidal wave, so that beautiful vapour became a dear friend, making me giddy and giggly and most of all, pain free.

I was examined by a doctor who indeed confirmed that I had collapsed from a bad case of sciatica. He asked how I had injured my back.

'I was cleaning under a table,' I lied. 'The dining room chairs were on the table and one fell off onto my back.'

This stupid, convoluted explanation was an obvious lie and he knew it.

Despite his suspicions that things weren't as they seemed, he prescribed Diazepam for the pain and gave me a pair of crutches for the walk home.

I tried to call and text Monica, but she wasn't answering me. When I returned home I waited in the room for her to come back from work hoping that, when she saw me on crutches, she would understand the severity of the situation.

When she did get home, she asked me what I was doing off work. I explained about my collapse and my hospital visit, careful not to blame her for any of it.

'Faker,' she snapped.

'I don't think so,' I said insulted. 'The doctor has signed me off work and I've got crutches for god sake.'

Monica snorted. 'Anyone can get crutches,' she said. 'You're faking, and if you're going to be off work, don't think I'm paying your way, I need my money.'

'I'm not going to ask you for anything,' I said.

'Good, cause if you can't afford to live here you'll have to move out.'

The coldness of her words hurt more than my back and as she walked out of the room I could have cried. I felt so alone at that moment, I couldn't really tell anyone what had happened or at least how. My family was miles away, I'd left my friends behind in Worcester when I'd moved to Hereford, I had no one.

I spent the next three weeks on crutches, Monica repeatedly saying that I was faking it and refusing to go out with me because *she would be embarrassed.*

After two weeks the insults and other derisory comments, started to subside. After three weeks the crutches were gone, but it took another two weeks of recuperation, including chiropractors and sciatic exercises, to get me fit enough for work again.

By the end of the five weeks, not only had the insults disappeared altogether, but I had a deeper insight into Monica's thinking.

We had discussed many things over the weeks and for once it was in a calm and peaceful manner. She told me that she wished that we had never moved into the shared house and that I should have been a man and got us a place to live, instead of taking the easy option. She also told me that she wanted me to be a father to her son and that she wanted us to be a family. Monica said that she wanted it to be we two and no other, a point I whole heartedly agreed with.

Slapping Monica had been suggested by Andreea and had turned out to be a disaster. My feeling now was that this advice had been given with the knowledge of exactly how Monica would react and Andreea's jealousy of me and Monica had led her to try and split us up. I believed that if we didn't get out of the house then Andreea would be the poison in the ear of Monica.

Our dream of a place of our own came sooner than we thought. Not long after I had returned to work, Monica's boss offered her a house to rent and we snapped his hand off.

Our own house. Our own life.

Things were about to get better.

"Until the end of time
I'll be there for you
You own my heart and mind
I truly adore you"

Prince

Moving in together was exciting. It was a new start away from the influences of Andreea, who I knew wanted to break me and Monica up, and Gabe, Monica's ex, who wanted her back.

Unfortunately, no sooner had we started our lives together in our new house than things started to go downhill fast, but this time, not because of fallouts and fights, but because of Monica's health.

Monica had told me that she had suffered from ingrowing pubic hair, this can be nasty and if one is not careful it can cause an infection than manifests itself in the form of a large painful lump in the genital area. She had told me how, while living in Romania, she had gotten said infection, the treatment for which is to cut out or lance the abscess which leaves an open wound; the wound is then packed with a dressing and then every day for the next several days the dressing is removed, pus is squeezed out of the wound and a clean dressing packed back into the hole.

The procedure is extremely painful. Pulling a packed dressing out of an open wound, the gauze dragging along the sides of raw flesh and then squeezing that wound is something no one should have to go through.

When it had happened in Romania the health care there was so bad that Monica had taken things into her own hands. Rather than put her trust in Romanian doctors she had gotten purposefully drunk one evening, heated a knife and operated on her own genitalia. She had slashed open the infection with the hot knife and squeezed out the pus, stuffing the wound with a dressing herself and treating herself for the next several days.

Now the infection was back, and Monica was in terrible pain. I pushed her to see a doctor, and at first, she resisted, insisting that things would be okay. I explained that this was not Romania and that, despite its failings, the NHS knew what they were doing.

A few days later she decided that I was right and made an appointment with her GP. On the morning of the appointment I insisted on going with her, my concern for *my Monica* was directly opposed to how calm and unconcerned she seemed to be.

Monica did not want me to go with her, whether it was because she was embarrassed or, maybe, she wasn't as cool as I thought, I don't know. Nevertheless, I was going with her. Even on the walk to the doctors she continued to tell me that she didn't want me with her, as I continued to insist she suddenly turned and punched me in the face. There were people all around us, most of whom stopped and stared, some of whom gasped at the random act of violence. As for me, I was too concerned for Monica to let that deter me and continued to follow her as if nothing had happened.

When we reached the doctors, Monica went in on her own, but when she came out after ten minutes, I knew something was wrong. Monica's face was ashen and, even though she tried to sound fine, there was uneasiness in her eyes.

'Christ,' I said, 'What's wrong?'

'I have to go to the hospital,' she said, 'now. Will you go with me?'

'Of course,' I said wrapping an arm around her.'

She was admitted immediately and moved onto a ward. I asked Monica if there was anything she needed and that evening I took her magazines, chocolates and sat with her until I was thrown out.

I spent that night alone in our new house just thinking about her, hoping she was okay. I loved her, adored her, and despite what had gone on before, I longed to grow old with her and watch our kids grow up together.

The next day I made my way to the hospital where I was told by a gruff receptionist that I would have to come back in visiting hours. I wanted, no, *needed,* to see my baby, so, undeterred, I exited the reception and laid out my plan. I returned a few minutes later and, sliding the door ajar, I slipped into the room staying low below the height of the reception desk. I crept forward watching the reflection of the receptionist in the glass of a poster on the opposite wall. There were a couple of older ladies sitting in reception and they laughed to themselves as I waited for my chance. As soon as I saw the receptionist turn her back I made a run for the ward. Monica's bed was the first through the door so as I entered, I rushed into her cubical and drew the curtains.

Monica wore no make-up, her face was pale and drawn, her hair lank and lifeless, yet I thought she was the most beautiful woman on the planet. I kissed her, a long, soft, lingering kiss filled with love.

'I missed you,' I said.

Monica laughed. 'You've only been without me a night,' she said.

'That's a night too long,' I replied kissing, her again.

The curtains pulled back and a nurse entered the cubical. I broke the kiss and stared at her with guilty eyes. The nurse gave Monica her pain killers and then turned to me.

'You shouldn't be here,' she said. 'Keep the curtains closed and don't make any noise.'

With a knowing smile she was gone, and I went back to kissing my girlfriend.

I went to see Monica several times over the next couple of days, sometimes in official visiting hours, sometimes using my stealth abilities.

She was eventually given the operation and the infection was cut away. However, now came the difficult and painful part.

I took her to the first doctor's appointment to have the dressing changed and the pus squeezed out of the wound. Monica laid down, the female doctor took hold of the dressing and started to pull. I had never heard another human being make the sound that came out of Monica's mouth, it was animalistic, raw and frightening.

The doctor stopped.

I could see by her face that Monica's cry of pain had scared even her.

'I think you should see another doctor,' she said.

My heart was pounding. I hated seeing Monica like this, if the doctor was scared, how scared was Monica.

'I think you should see another GP,' the doctor reiterated. 'I don't want to hurt you.'

Monica sat up and pulled on her clothes. She smiled at the doctor and said, 'Give me the dressings, I'll do it myself.'

"I'm knitting with only one needle
Unravelling fast it's true
I'm driving only three wheels these days
But my dear, how about you?
I'm going slightly mad..."

Queen

I knew that Monica's rehabilitation would take time, after all, every evening she would torture herself changing the dressing, squeezing out pus, cleaning and redressing the wound. I also knew that, because she was in so much pain, that I would be the target of any built-up angst, and I was prepared for that, and I accepted that – for love, one will do almost anything.

The problem arose after the wound had healed and recovery was over, the *taking it out on me* did not go away. She was annoyed with me all the time, I trod carefully around her as much as I could, but it was difficult not to show my frustration. We were in our own house now so what was the problem? Well, I soon found out.

The problem was that the new home had been found by Monica not me. In Monica's eyes, this was another example of my lack of manliness. She was the provider and I was…what? Nothing. A hanger on?

Monica called me lazy, accused me once again of not caring, of only loving sex not her, not valuing her, not being worthy of *'the beautiful woman you have in your bed'*. I felt guilty and confused, I didn't know what I could do and if I asked Monica what she wanted, her answer was always the same:

'You figure it out. Be a man for fuck sake.'

Maybe men were different in Romania, but I was English, relationships were supposed to be negotiations, compromise, but no, I had to be a certain way.

'Even fucking Lizzie got tired of you,' she told me. 'No one is ever going to want you. You can't support anyone, I have to support you.'

She was right, I had let her down again. I was just continuing to fail at every turn. I couldn't do anything right. I needed to sort myself out, make the girl happy for Christ's sake. But each time I tried I got it wrong, I was such a fucking loser. Why was this amazing woman with me?

Then one night she came in from work. I greeted her cheerfully and went to kiss her, but she brushed me aside. I tried to speak to her, but she would not communicate at all.

As I've said, I hate being ignored, I would rather fight than be ignored as nothing is aired and it bottles up, but she refused to communicate.

I went to bed to get away from her and, stupid as it was, I knocked things on the floor on purpose. I did this in an attempt to make a noise so that Monica would investigate, to get some reaction, some dialogue even.

Nothing.

The next day was worse. It began with silence, just as the night before, but I could see that she had something to say. I tried to ignore it, hoping it would pass, but eventually she cracked.

'I fucking hate you,' she said. 'I can't bear to be with you anymore.'

Then she trotted out the classics once more, *'Piece of shit'*, *'you don't love me'*, *'you ruined my life'*, *'you don't give me peace'*. However, she used those lines so many times I had become desensitised to them, they were nothing but noise.

'You're nothing,' she said, 'just an old man.'

This new line cut me inside and she knew it.

'Why would I want to be with someone like you,' she said, taking advantage while I was still reeling from the *old man* comment.

I shouted at her now, the pain, the anger, the desperation for her to love me the way I loved her was just overflowing.

This was what she needed. The screaming began an exchange of insults, hers clever and targeted, designed for maximum impact, mine loose and weak, a babbling mess that went nowhere.

She spat in my face again, more controlled than last time. Spittle ran down my face as she threw more venom at me. She punched me, a head shot, a good one, catching me in the temple and sending my brain spinning. She followed that up with another and another.

'I hate you!' She screamed. 'I want to stab you in the eye!'

I ran into the kitchen, my heart near bursting with anxiety. I snatched open the drawer and pulled out a large kitchen knife and went back to her.

'Here,' I said handing her the knife, 'do it.'

She refused to take it, backing away, calling me a cunt.

'Stab me!' I shouted. 'Get it over with.'

Monica pushed past me and ran into the living room. She punched her own head.

'I want to die, you make me want to die.'

I don't know what came over me, my brain had shut down and stress and anxiety had taken over.

'You don't want to die,' I said. 'I want to fucking die.'

I took the knife and slashed my hand.

'You want rid of me? You want to be free of me?'

I cut my hand again and again, blood ran down my hand and arm.

'Don't bleed on the carpet,' she said angrily, 'this is not our house.'

I couldn't believe her. I cut myself again, but even in the state I was in I grabbed a tea towel so I would indeed not bleed on the carpet.

Monica grabbed her phone. 'I'm calling the police,' she said.

'Call them,' I shouted. 'Go on, tell them what you're like.'

Monica called 999 and spoke to the police. She told them that we had had a fight and that I had cut myself. This was a woman in distress blaming everything on her mental boyfriend and the police lapped it up.

Two police officers and an ambulance were at the house within minutes. They took Monica outside and then proceeded to question me for half an hour. In the meantime, they had taken Monica outside and let her go on her way.

I tried to explain to the officers what had really happened, but they were too concerned with her side of things and 'keeping her safe'. I explained that Monica had hit me, spat in my face, threatened to stab me in the eye. I told them that I had cut myself to feel something, anything but the pain I was in inside.

'Okay sir, as long as you are okay now,' he said.

They ignored everything that I had said, didn't hear a damn thing.

Later that evening I heard the key in the door. I tried to be calm and called, 'Hello.'

No answer.

I heard voices and went to investigate. Monica had arrived with Andreea and they had garbage bags.

My stomach churned as she started to pack all the stuff she could. She wouldn't talk to me, only to say she was leaving me and that I had two days to get out of the house.

I was confused and hurt, I didn't know what to do or say, some of my words were loving, some harsh, but none of them were much louder than a whisper.

They worked together packing, what they could while I paced downstairs desperate to stop her leaving, but not knowing how.

I called my friend Wayne and told him what had happened.

'Let her go,' he told me. 'This is no good for either of you. You'll be okay.'

This was what should be said, but not what I wanted to hear. I wanted to hear solutions not sense. I wanted to hear how I could put this right, not how breaking up was the right thing to do.

When she was ready to leave she didn't even say goodbye. I looked out of the upstairs window and saw Gabe, her ex, helping load his car.

She had told me I had two days to get out, but I had nowhere to go. It was obvious that Monica was going back to the shared house, but I could not, obviously.

I called my friend Tara and spent the next half hour crying.

'I love her,' I told Tara. I told her what I'd been through, but still, I didn't want to lose her.

'But, John, look what she's done,' she said. 'If a guy hit me what would you say?'

'I'd tell you to get out of there,' I said honestly, 'before I came to London to smack him one.'

'Well then, take your own advice,' she said. 'I don't want to see you hurt.'

Then I made another phone call. I called the only person who I knew could help me.

'Hi Lizzie,' I said. 'Can you do me a huge favour?'

"I know your eyes in the morning sun
I feel you touch me in the pouring rain
And the moment that you wander far from me
I want to feel you in my arms again"

Bee Gees

My friend, Ray, drove from Birmingham and we loaded my stuff into his car and he drove me to Worcester. I tried to talk to him, about everything that had gone on, but although Ray had always been there for me as he was now, I think he was uncomfortable with the whole situation and didn't know what to say.

I unloaded my stuff when I got to Lizzie's and when Ray had gone I told her everything that had happened. She had every right not to help me, I had left her some time before, hurt her deeply and now I was begging for a place to stay. Lizzie was an amazing human being, that was obvious.

Over the next week Lizzie saw me both quiet and upset, I spent my days commuting to Hereford for my job or wandering the streets of Worcester, my head hung low, mentally kicking myself for chasing away the love of my life. I spent my nights feeling the same, but at night the tears flowed.

Lizzie was in an awkward situation, she didn't know what to say to me and even if she did, why should she comfort me?

I had not drunk for fourteen years, but I felt like it now. I wanted to drown out the hurt I was feeling, drown out the thought of how stupid I had been to let this happen, fill the hole I had inside with alcohol, cool anesthetising alcohol.

My mind threw up scenario after scenario of what I could have and should have done better. I should have gotten us a place to live, I should have given Monica the peace she required, I should have been the man she wanted, needed even.

I called her and spoke to her, cried and begged for her to come back to me. Her voice was cold with a steely edge, I could hear Andreea in the background every time I called, and I knew she was playing Claudius to Monica's Hamlet – *She poisons her i' th' garden for 's estate.*

I needed to talk to Monica without bloody *Mary Ann Cotton* lurking in the background and I tried several times before I did get her alone.

'I'm sorry,' I said over and over. 'I don't want to live without you. You mean everything to me.'

'You can't keep behaving like you do, John,' she said. 'I can't take it. I don't think that you are good for me.'

'Meet me,' I implored. 'Let me come to you and we can talk.'

Monica was silent for what seemed like forever. 'I will come to Worcester,' she said. 'I'll come, but we will only talk. I don't want to get back together.'

We made a date and time and I was hopeful of the outcome. I wanted her back, I needed her, I couldn't imagine me without her.

I was waiting when she arrived at the station. My god, she looked amazing. She was wearing black jeans with the fitted striped shirt that I liked so much, unbuttoned just enough to show me what I was missing.

I threw my arms around her, tears were already forming in my eyes, and when I kissed her, I was overjoyed that she kissed me back. She pulled backed from the kiss and wiped a tear away from my eye with a finger.

'Come on, stop this,' she said sweetly. 'Let's go get a drink and talk.'

I took her to a bar owned by my friend Ali. Ali served us himself.

'Choose whatever you want,' he told us, 'it's on me.'

Monica looked up at him. 'Why?' She asked suspiciously.

'Because John is a friend,' Ali replied. 'John is a great guy.'

We ordered strawberry daiquiris, a virgin one for me, and I looked at my Monica, falling in love all over again.

'I can't do this,' she told me. 'It's just too hard.'

'Give me another chance,' I asked. 'It will be better, I promise. I want to be the man you want me to be.'

'Where are you staying?' She said, changing the subject for now.

I sipped at my cocktail trying to think what to say. If I told her that I was staying at Lizzie's, then I may as well say goodnight and goodbye here and now.

'I'm staying with a friend, Liam.'

Liam was a radio DJ I'd known for some years.

'Oh,' she said. 'He's okay with you staying there?'

'Yes,' I said, 'for now. But I don't want to stay there, I want to be with you.'

'John...'

'I'll get us a place,' I said, desperation rising in my voice. 'Stay where you are for now and let me get us a flat.'

Monica looked at me over the brim of her glass. 'I don't know.'

'If I fuck up again you can leave and never look back. I promise things will be better, I'll be better.'

Monica was silent again.

'Please,' I said.

'Okay,' she said eventually. 'You have to be a better person, you have to show me.'

'I will,' I said, 'promise.'

I walked her back to the station feeling a million dollars. I couldn't believe my pain was over. As I put her on the train I promised again to get us a flat and that I would be a better man.

'I love you,' I said as the train pulled away.

'I love you,' she said.

Now the difficult job of telling Lizzie it was back on again with Monica.

"I never hide the feelings inside
And though I'm standing with my back to the wall
I know that even in a summer love
A little bit of rain must fall"

Whitesnake

Lizzie had not reacted much upon my confession that me and Monica were back together, beyond an acknowledgement and a disapproving look. I don't know what she was feeling inside, but if it was any different from her exterior then she was a damn good actor.

My mum and dad were more judgmental, telling me that I was a fool, but that, *'It's your life, son.'* My mum admitted that she was scared of me and Monica getting back together, she said that she was afraid that Monica would use a weapon on me or that she would push me too far and I would hurt her.

I tried to explain that, although Monica had been violent, she had problems that I was willing to help with, and that I had to take most of the blame as I had not been the man she wanted me to be.

'Things will be better now,' I assured her.

My mum did not hold the same optimism.

My first move was to find us a flat and for that I needed money, something I didn't have. I found two flats, both of which were perfect for different reasons. The first was a brand new, one-bedroom apartment that had built in wardrobes and a sunken living room. It was kinda cramped, however, and the kitchen looked as if it was just plonked in the middle of the hallway…very strange.

The second was a two-bedroom, top floor flat with a large living room, big double bedroom and separate kitchen with a tiny annex for a washing machine.

I loved both, but the initial expense was out of my price range, so I turned to work to help. After much negotiation and plenty of posturing on their part and bragging about how good they were to me, they advanced me £600 to be paid back in £200 instalments straight from my wages. Now I had the cash and two choices of apartment.

I spent the night with Monica in a local hotel and as well as the usual activities, we talked about the apartments. I asked her to come and see both places with me so she could help me make up my mind.

'Jesus Christ, John,' she said. 'Can't you just be a man about this.'

I was being weak again and I couldn't do that. I just wanted her to be a part of the decision-making process, I didn't want her to be disappointed.

So, I did what she asked and was *a man* about it, choosing the two-bedroom flat. I won Brownie points for saying my reasoning was so that her son could come and stay, which went down very well.

I arranged everything. I moved heaven and earth to get the place ready for Monica as quickly as possible, but it still wasn't as quickly as I wanted it.

The day before Monica moved in I spent the night there to clean the place and ready it for her. I slept on the floor as we had no furniture, but I didn't sleep much, I was too hyped about this being a fresh start and the start of me being a new man. I knew what I had to do, and I had a plan how to do it. I acknowledged that things wouldn't be perfect, that there would be fights and possibly violence, but I also knew that she couldn't help it, and that I was there to help her through it. I had worked in care with severe challenging behaviour for years and seen all types of violence from self-injurious behaviour, to clients attacking me. Monica was no different, different problems, but all in all it was the same – it wasn't her fault, and like my support worker role, I was there to help.

I had arranged for a removal van to collect Monica and her belongings the next morning, and I awaited her arrival, excited for her to see our new home. I felt like a teenager with the butterflies and the whole embarrassing she-bang. I had not felt this way when me and Lizzie moved into our permanent home as the house was left to us by her parents when they moved to Spain, which many people say I was lucky to be living mortgage free, but I hated that damn house from day one.

This was different. I was, and still am, terrible at DIY, so renting is perfect, anything goes wrong and the landlord fixes it. The downside, of course, is that it would never be mine, but I could live with that.

Monica arrived later that morning and, as the movers offloaded her stuff, she took a look around the apartment – and she loved it.

She threw her arms around my neck and kissed me releasing me as the movers brought in the bed. She took over then, and I smiled as I watched her direct the movers, telling them where stuff should go and to be careful every now and then.

I had a good feeling about *this* time.

When everything had been brought inside we paid the movers and Monica took another tour of the place. She started to decorate in her head.

'We need to get a canvas for this wall,' she said, about the space over the bed. 'We'll have to go into town and get a washing machine and we'll need to go food shopping.'

She walked into the living room where most of the items had been placed.

'And this will need sorting and putting away.'

I stopped her by pulling her close and kissing her.

'Welcome to *our* home future Mrs. James,' I said.

Monica smiled and kissed me again, and before we knew it we were making love on top of our belongings.

"Sweet wonderful you

You make me feel happy with the things you do

Oh, can it be so

This feeling follows me wherever I go"

Fleetwood Mac

This was the life.

Monica was far enough away from the influence of Andreea and Gabe and, even if she saw them now and then, she seemed to be happy enough with me and our apartment.

Our place was also closer to work for both of us, so if we finished before the other, or if it was our day off, we would meet the other from work just to walk home together.

I happily reported our success to my parents who were still wary saying to watch out for any change in her behaviour. I scoffed at the little faith they had, I was enjoying life again, could they not be happy for me instead of looking for signs of trouble?

To help Monica, I began to read about personality disorders and found that *Borderline Personality Disorder* was a close match to Monica's past behaviour. Of course, I did not tell her this at first, as I did not want to upset her, but it was interesting, and I learned how to live with it.

Monica did try to start an argument several times, but I remained calm and used *positive language* in a *non-threatening tone*.

I used *active listening* and would say things like, 'I hear what you're saying,' and, 'we can work on that.' Even in the face of criticism I was calm and positive. The results were amazing. Any build-up of emotion that Monica displayed, dissolved as quickly as it had appeared.

I even cut my hair for her. I'd had long hair that went to the middle of my back for years, but Monica had recently taken a dislike to it, so I cut it. The reaction was just what I'd hoped for, a beaming smile, a jump into my arms, a thankful kiss. Amazing.

Life was as it should be, and we again started to make plans for a baby. I wanted a child so damn much that it tore me apart inside every time Monica told me that her period had started. I cursed myself for not being able to make her pregnant. Why couldn't I have a kid?

I suggested adoption to Monica, but she rejected the idea immediately. She was determined to have a child with me – *our* child.

The diary came out once more, and the sex became planned around it. I didn't like this routine, but if I wanted a child then I would do anything, literally anything – I would have sold my soul for a daughter of our own.

Things weren't always perfect between us, there were spats of fighting, cruel words and the playing returned with a new way of hurting me. Monica would sit next to me on the sofa and put her feet up on my lap, once there I would massage her feet and she would move them on my lap digging her heel into my groin. At first, I made the mistake of crying out in pain, but after Monica had stormed off to bed one night calling me a pussy, I didn't complain again.

I took the cruel words and the kicks to the crutch, because I didn't want to lose her again and when I didn't react, she was the Monica I wanted – sort of.

I even changed my ways to suit how Monica liked to do things. I had always been a *free spirit* kinda guy.

I would do the laundry when I wanted, and housework when I wanted, but Monica was so organised, so, no trips to the coffee shop on the morning of our weekends off, it was housework time.

Monica would get mad if I even suggested going out before the cleaning had been done, and it had to be done in a certain way, no slacking.

Laundry in, the bathroom cleaned, the kitchen scrubbed, the sides polished, the carpet hoovered, the bathroom and kitchen mopped, the mirrors sparkling. Only after all this had been done to her high standard, could I even think about going out, and if I was allowed to go out without admonishment, I would have to go on my own, Monica often preferring to stay at home and play video games. Sometimes, I would stay at home because of the look I received when suggesting a coffee. I got very good at spotting *the look* and modified my behaviour accordingly. Sometimes I could get it wrong, however. This was the case when I went to the coffee shop one morning and had failed to notice the subtle signs of displeasure.

When I got there, I had taken but a sip of coffee, when I received a call from Monica.

'Hey, baby,' I said on answering.

What I got in return was a tirade of shouted obscenities and insults. I left my coffee and went home knowing I had screwed up.

I was so happy.

The days, weeks and months slipped by without major incident and I grew more and more confident that we could make it. I had even begun divorce proceedings and was only stopped when I found out how expensive it was. I explained to Monica that I would have to save for it which didn't go down well, and I could understand her disappointment, I could. She told me that I must be wasting my money as she was paying half of everything so where did my money go? It was her that was losing out, her that had no money to send home to Romania.

Truth was, that Monica was not paying half of everything. Monica's contribution was a little more than half the rent so with internet charges, phone line charges, gas, electric, water, council tax, TV licence and on and on, her money hardly covered a thing.

And as for her being in monetary deprivation, she dropped her phone, actually, she threw it to the floor in anger, and smashed the screen and, while the phone was sent off for repair, she turned down an offer of my spare phone in order to buy a brand new one for over £500...her broken phone was returned, mended, in three days.

But okay, I was the man, I was the bread winner, she was the mum trying to support her eighteen-year-old son in Romania, I get it. I tried, I really did. Every time I tried to put money away there was another bill through the door, and I couldn't discuss the bills either as this too would make her mad, but she did have her son on her mind so okay, that was fine.

Other than these little niggly matters things were great. I was in love and happy and I was sure that everything would work out fine. I just had to try harder that was all.

A part of me trying to make her happy was letting her decorate the flat. Monica hung flowery canvasses that she had bought from the charity shop and bought a dressing table and wardrobe. The wardrobe we shared, but Monica didn't like that fact, so I was relegated to a small place on one side of the double wardrobe and one piece of the shelf. She also bought home a chest of drawers that she had been given at work after the owner had died. That too was hers, and I was allowed one drawer out of four.

I secretly hated everything she had done to the place, but, acceptance was all a part of me making her happy, and it worked. Monica was happy with my silence and non-confrontational style, and I was happy that she was happy.

Life was great, honestly it was.

"I'm so in love with you

Whatever you want to do

Is all right with me

Cause you make me feel brand new

And I want to spend my life with you"

Al Green

'Oh, sweet god.'

I sunk into my pillow and waited while the euphoria wore off. My head eventually stopped spinning and the world righted itself once more.

'You make me feel amazing,' I said to Monica and she climbed off me.

'I wish you'd be on top more you lazy bastard,' she said.

I laughed.

'I'm not kidding,' she said falling into bed beside me and wrapping her arm around my waist patting my stomach. 'Fatty.'

I ignored the name calling. 'I'll do it any way you want, babe,' I told her. 'What do you want? Tell me something kinky.'

'Rape me,' she said. 'I love your strength, hold me down and take me.'

I laughed again. 'Really?'

'Yeh.'

'That wouldn't be making love,' I told her.

'So? Sometimes I like to make love, sometimes I like to be fucked,' she said without humour.

Half of me was aroused by what she was saying and half of me concerned.

'We'd have to have a safe word,' I said.

'*Fuck off*, that good enough?' Now she did laugh, and so did I.

I loved to hear Monica laugh, I'd heard it a lot in the beginning of the relationship. I remembered hanging clothes on the line with her and I took all the pegs and clipped them to her hair, her head becoming a mass of coloured plastic. We couldn't breathe for laughing that day. I couldn't do that now without having my head bit off.

'I love you,' I told her for the millionth time that morning.

'I love you,' she told me pulling me closer. She took my hand and placed it on her belly. 'Don't you wish that there was a baby in there?'

My heart swelled to hear that and then sank in the knowledge that there was no baby.

'Do you think we'll ever have a baby?' I asked.

'I don't know,' she said, 'but I want your baby more than anything in the world, and want to marry you and grow old with you and put you in a nursing home when you have dementia.'

'Cheeky bitch,' I said laughing.

'I'll bring my new boyfriend to see you but you won't care cause you won't know who I am.'

'New boyfriend?' I said. 'You'll be old too, so he'll be a grandad.'

'No,' she said laughing and poking me, 'because it won't be long until you get dementia, I'm a lot younger than you remember.'

We both laid back and laughed until our sides hurt.

Monica got out of bed and went to the bathroom while I waited in bed, a stupid great grin on my face. I waited and waited, but she didn't come back. She had taken her phone with her and I knew she would be sitting on the toilet playing that stupid game that had started to take over a lot of her time. After a while I got up and went to see what she was doing. As I reached the bathroom the door opened, and Monica came out, her face expressionless.

'You okay?' I asked,

She looked at me with eyes full of hate.

'What?' I said.

'Leave me alone,' she mumbled.

'Sorry?' I was confused again now. 'You are looking at me like you can't stand being in the same space as me.'

'I can't,' she said.

My stomach started to turn over. We had had such a good time in bed both making love and laughing and now?

'But…but, I haven't done anything,' I said, my voice meek.

'I know you haven't,' she said. 'Just leave me alone, don't speak to me.'

I touched her arm as she started to walk away. 'This isn't fair,' I said, 'I've not done anything wrong.'

'Leave me alone!' she said, raising her voice.

I shook my head. I didn't want another fight, especially when I didn't know what had started this.

'I'm going out,' I told her.

'Then go,' she said.

I got dressed and went out without saying another word. I sat in the coffee shop for over an hour, my head spinning with the strange morning I'd had.

When I did return to the apartment Monica was in bed watching a movie.

'You okay?' I asked. 'Are we okay?'

'You're such a fucking idiot,' she said tapping the bed for me to get in.

'Why?'

'You need to give me a couple of minutes then come to me and hold me,' she said, as I slid in next to her.

'How am I supposed to know that?'

Monica sighed heavily. 'You just know.'

'I'm not a mind reader,' I said. 'I can't tell what you need from me.'

'Well you should,' she said, in all seriousness.

I didn't know how to answer that and my head was flicking through a rolodex of things to say and rejecting every answer I came across, so I kissed her.

Things progressed quickly until Monica told me to stop, but the *stop* was not a command but playful and I knew what she wanted, this was my chance to get our day back on track.

I held her firmly as she fought against me, her porn star acting getting into full rhythm with her head lashing from side to side.

'No, stop, no.'

She sighed and writhed and pushed against my hands.

I held her down just as she wanted, listening carefully for the 'fuck off' safe word, but it never came.

Soon we were making love and then...I did the stupidest thing...I stopped.

I climbed off her and she sat bolt upright.

'Why did you stop?' she demanded to know.

'I just wanted to prove I could hold you down,' I said.

Jesus Christ, I don't even know where that came from, it was such a stupid thing to do and say.

Monica jumped up, fury burning in her eyes.

'You fucking bastard,' she screamed.

She punched me in the chest – which I guess I deserved – then she punched me again and again.

'Get the fuck away from me,' I shouted and curled up in a ball on the bed.

'I can't believe it,' she said, 'you raped me.'

Now it was my turn to sit bolt upright. 'You know that's not true,' I said.

'Stay away from me,' she said holding herself. 'You raped me. I should call the police, you raped me.'

Monica grabbed her dressing gown and went into the spare room. I climbed into bed and pulled the covers tightly around me.

'Oh my god,' I thought, *'oh my god.'*

"Buckets of rain

Buckets of tears

Got those buckets comin' out of my ears"

Bob Dylan

The next day things returned to relative normality, at least for Monica. That "R" word was still in my head. How could she say that? I knew that she had been angry about my 'joke', but Jesus.

The accusation of rape really fucked with my head. Outwardly I tried to behave like nothing had happened, I could not bear the thought of another fight. Inwardly, however, I was a mess. I ran the love making over and over and over in my head trying to figure out if I had actually done what she said. I was scared and hurt and my mind was screaming, my heart shrivelling. I kept waiting for Monica to call the police, but she didn't.

The whole episode affected my love making, I was extremely self-aware, there was no enjoyment for me anymore, it was all show, all for Monica. During sex, I would ask her again and again if she was okay, but that would only make Monica frustrated until she would tell me to shut up.

I tried to avoid arguments, but when they did occur Monica had a new battle cry:

'I'm scared of you.'

She even told me that she had gone to work and told her colleagues, 'If I don't come into work and don't phone in sick, call the police, my boyfriend would have killed me.'

As a result, my stature became diminutive, my voice softer and my body language small and minimal. When an argument did flare up, I was quick to apologise, it didn't matter whether I knew what I was apologising for or not, I just needed the fight to end quickly.

Monica even demanded I follow her to the bathroom one afternoon and tore me a new one with a five-minute shouted rant, because I left the toilet lid down.

'You are supposed to leave the toilet seat down but the lid up!' She screamed. 'I need to be able to come in and sit down on the toilet without lifting the lid. You selfish cunt. You don't respect me.'

'I'm sorry,' I said, 'I'll remember.'

On the flip side, there were nights when I would come home from work and be greeted by an excited Monica.

'Babyyyyyyyyy,' she'd scream and leap into my arms covering my face in kisses.

It was like swimming in a black pool of misery and hurt, only for Monica to yank me up into the sunshine of love before throwing me back into the darkness.

I was walking on eggshells constantly, I didn't know which Monica I would come home to.

Scared Monica: 'You frighten me, John.'

Loving Monica: 'I can't wait to marry you, you're the only man I ever want.'

Silent Monica: 'Leave me alone, I don't want to speak to you.'

My anxiety levels were through the roof and I spent days on end hoping that she would be involved in a fatal accident. Her death seemed like my only way out, I could not stand the thought of being with her when she was hateful and more than that, the thought of her leaving me drove me to distraction. Monica's death by fatal accident seemed like the only way I would get everything I needed to escape this.

My stress was affecting my work life in a big way. I became more and more frustrated with both staff and clients.

I had worked with severe challenging behaviour for years and had always been calm and patient even when getting punched and kicked and spat at, but now my home life was mirroring work, and the frustration from my personal life directly impacted on it.

The crucial point came when I was supporting a client that was physically challenging and needed two staff to be with him. My colleague had disappeared to god knows where, leaving me with the client on my own.

The client began to get frustrated and started to be challenging. I tried to protect myself by taking his hands and following the protocols that were in place. Suddenly, the client smacked me in the side of the head with his fist. Involuntarily I clenched my fist. It went no further than a clench, but I knew that I was a small step away from losing my career and worse.

That evening I sat at home and went over my day. It didn't matter how I tried to justify it, the fact remained, that my stress and anxiety had gotten the better of me and I could not allow that to happen.

I grabbed my phone, took a deep breath and fired off an email to my boss. The email was a long-winded explanation of my decision, but if I was to be succinct, I could whittle the email to two words:

'I quit.'

"I hurt myself today
To see if I still feel
I focus on the pain
The only things that's real"

Johnny Cash

Monica once again showed that she could play all parts. When I told her that I had quit my job she was, at first, very supportive.

'You hated that job anyway,' she said. 'You're damn good at your job, you'll get another one easy. Join an agency.'

I was glad she felt that way, or, for the short time she did feel that way, as less than an hour later she was questioning why I'd quit.

'Why did you quit? Why just like that?' She asked suspicious.

'I told you why,' I said. 'I was seconds away from assaulting a client and I'd never work in care again.'

'No,' she said frowning, 'There's something you're not saying.'

'Sorry?'

'Something's gone on,' she said. 'What really happened?'

'I told you,' I said.

'I don't believe you.' Then, 'Nobody liked you anyway, I bet everybody is glad that you quit.'

I ignored the remarks, at least outwardly.

Being out of the place I had been working at was a relief somewhat, the stress was limited to home now, but still, that had to be dealt with. I did, however, follow her advice and joined an agency.

I also had a concert coming up. I had tickets for Whitesnake, a band that both me and Monica loved, but Monica had told me that she didn't want to go, even though the tickets had cost me £50 or more, it meant nothing to her and, more to the point, she had made it clear that she didn't want *me* to go either.

As the gig drew closer I began to get anxious, I wanted to go, but I didn't want a fall out again. I called my mum and told her that I was going to go to a concert, but I was telling Monica that I was going to a family funeral and I asked my mum to back me up on that if Monica was to mention anything.

My mum was beyond frustrated with me.

'John, this is not a healthy relationship,' she said. 'You have to lie to go to a concert? You never had to lie to Lizzie.'

'Look, mum,' I said, 'can you do this for me please? I'm with Monica now and I just don't want us to argue.'

'She's not good for you, John,' she told me. 'Please, this is not healthy.'

'Will you do it or not?' I snapped.

My mum was silent for a few seconds before sighing heavily. 'Okay,' she said. 'I'll do it, but I don't agree with it.'

'Fine, thanks,' I said before putting down the phone.

A week later I went to Cardiff to see Whitesnake. I called Monica after the show to tell her all about the fictional funeral. She was sympathetic, and our conversation was filled with 'I love you'. I remember thinking I should go to more fictional funerals if it softened Monica as this had.

When I returned the next day, Monica asked me again how the *funeral* had gone and said that she was sorry that I had missed the Whitesnake concert. She did this several times and I got the suspicion that she knew I had lied and was waiting for me to confess. I was no fool, I knew that a confession would cause me to suffer her wrath, so I was intelligent enough to keep my mouth shut.

The hot and cold of Monica's behaviour continued, she kept me on my toes not knowing which Monica was going to be waiting for me at home. Even in the morning, I did not know whether to speak or not. Monica would sometimes snap at me to leave her alone some mornings, on others, if I did not speak she would say that I was ignoring her. If I was on an afternoon shift I would still get up at 5am and make Monica a cup of tea before going to work, but even this act of kindness had to be well measured as her mood could mean an argument could start the day if I didn't play it right.

Sometimes I would awake with Monica's hand inside my pyjama pants and before I was fully awake we were having sex; on other mornings I would wake aroused and begin to touch her, only to get slapped away and told I was a fucking idiot.

Night-time was the same. I never knew how to conduct myself in bed, did I hold her or turn over and go to sleep, did I try and make love to her or did I wait for her to lead the way – it was all very confusing.

One evening we climbed into bed together and I held her close. I began stroking her back and became aroused. I started to touch her, and she leapt out of bed.

'Fuck. I'm sick of this.'

'Sick of what?' I asked.

'Is fucking me all you think about?' She said, starting to cry. 'All my life men have just wanted me to fuck me, I thought you were different.'

'I'm sorry,' I said climbing out of bed and holding her. 'I'm so sorry, you aren't just an object to me, I love you. Please, I won't try anything unless you want me to. I'm sorry.'

For the next several nights I never even held her unless she asked me to. I was scared to even get aroused and even felt guilty about fancying her.

About a week later I was holding her on request and she began to sigh heavily.

'I'm going into the other room,' she said, getting out of bed and throwing on her dressing gown.

'What have I done?' I asked, knowing it was my fault.

'When you want to fuck it's okay, but now you just lie there…breathing.'

I sat up in bed feeling guilty and, again, not knowing why. 'Breathing? What do you mean?'

Monica did an impression of Darth Vader's raspy breath.

'I'm lying there waiting for you to touch me and you lie there like a fucking idiot breathing in the back of my neck.'

I swallowed my annoyance. 'How am I supposed to know when you want me and when you don't?' I said.

'You should know,' she said. 'Any decent man would know.'

'I'm not a mind reader,' I said.

But Monica had already left the room.

"Love hurts

Love scars

Love wounds and marks"

Nazareth

Love is like a cloud, it holds a lot of rain, and the cloud above my head was ready for a full-on thunderstorm.

I had never been more confused about love. I wanted Monica like I'd never wanted anyone in my life, but I hated her in equal measure...okay, not in equal measure, my love for her was strong as hell and it filled me with literal fear to think of me being without her, but I did wonder why.

It wasn't just the *playing* or the fighting or the silence she forced upon me whenever she felt like it, but the guilt I felt for her every mood. I also spent a lot of time questioning my own reality. Monica seemed to tell me one thing one day and the opposite thing the next. I never knew if I had misheard, whether my mind was making shit up, or whether she was actually contradictory.

She had also increased her rhetoric that she was scared of me too. If we argued and I raised my voice she would back away, cower even; she ran into the bedroom when I called her a bitch and shut the door jamming a chair against it. It was over the top drama, but it made me feel guilty.

Our arguments became one sided, she would shout and scream and call me every name under the sun, and I would begin to shout only for it to turn into a whimper. I was apologising a lot more now too, her threats to leave me were a main ingredient in every row.

She even sat me down one time and told me in a manner that was ice cold, that she needed to leave me and that I was no good for her. She told me that I had ruined her life and that I was not supportive of her or her son. Monica said that since being with me she had nothing.

'What do you want?' I asked, 'My wallet?'

'What? Who the fuck said anything about your wallet, but you give me nothing. You don't support me. I need someone to look after me, to look after my son. I have not sent any money home in months, because of you.'

I was astonished. I had never, and would never, stop her from sending money home. Monica earned more than me and was not paying half the housekeeping, so the facts of the matter didn't add up.

She ranted at me for eleven minutes, I can be this precise as I recorded the conversation on my phone and when listening to it back, I was horrified at how weak my own voice is, how pathetic I sound.

I WhatsApp'd my friend, Wayne, the recording and he sent a message back eleven minutes later.

'Bud, you have to kick the bitch to the curb,' he said. 'Fucking dump her, mate. She's evil, pure fucking evil. I can't believe you let her speak to you like that, and to use her son against you...pure evil.'

I sat alone that night after Monica had gone to bed and cried. I wanted Monica back, my Monica, the Monica that I'd fallen in love with.

The arguments became a daily occurrence and my mind began to fracture. During one particular argument, the reason for which remains a mystery, she stood before me screaming the usual insults and I took them stone faced and unaffected. Monica tried again and again to get me to respond but I'd heard it all before.

Then. 'I don't love you,' she said.

My face must have twitched, showed some level of hurt.

'Aaaahhhhh,' she said, and smiled.

She knew she had me but did not expect my response.

'Get the fuck out,' I said.

'What?' She asked showing emotion of her own.

'Get out of *my* flat.'

'So it's your fucking flat?'

'My name on the lease, my flat, get the fuck out!'

Monica started to pack, but there was apprehension in her actions. She had never seen me like this and I had never felt like this, enough was enough.

I watched her pack her things, anger burning in my chest. All the things she'd done, all the things she had said, all the pain I had been through.

Monica went into the spare room to pack more things and I went into the bedroom and snatched up her keys from the bedside cabinet. I removed the key to the flat and threw the rest onto the bed.

'I've taken your fucking key back,' I called out.

I heard a crash and then another and then another.

I went into the kitchen where the sound was coming from. Monica was standing on the opposite side of the kitchen, her face red with anger, her eyes black spheres, shards of broken cups and plates were strewn across the floor.

'You fucking bastard,' she screamed at me.

She picked up the cafeteria I had bought a few weeks before and smashed it against the work surface sending up a spray of glass.

I grabbed a mug from the side. 'You want to smash shit? I can smash shit.'

I threw the mug on the floor and watched as it bounced, not even a chip.

I picked up the mug again. 'We can all smash shit,' I said, throwing the mug down again.

Again, it bounced, again not even a chip.

It took another three throws before the mug broke and by this time Monica had left the kitchen.

When I went after her she was standing in the hallway, arms crossed defiantly across her chest.

'Get out,' I demanded.

'Fuck you,' she spat.

I went to grab her by the arm to physically throw her out but, as soon as I touched her, she attacked me.

Monica punched me in the face and several blows to the body. I tried to back away but she grabbed the collar of my jumper and jerked me back to hit me again. She twisted her hand in my hair pulling my head down and planting several upper cuts into my face, all the time screaming like some crazy animal.

I twisted and turned and eventually broke free. I ran into the bedroom, scooped up her belongings and carried them downstairs throwing them out of the door.

'Follow them, bitch,' I told her.

Monica hesitated and then reluctantly left the flat.

As soon as she was out, I quickly threw some of my own clothes into a bag and was going to go to my parents, I needed a break from this madness. I stopped on the way out and took some photos of my wrecked kitchen and headed out.

I locked the door behind me and as I passed Monica on the street calling for a taxi, I said, 'Psycho.'

"Take away the sensation inside

Bitter sweet migraine in my head

It's like a throbbing toothache in my mind..."

Green Day

In the following twenty-four hours after throwing Monica out I felt stronger than I'd ever felt. I called Lizzie and told her I was free, I text Wayne and told him I was rid of her, I called my friend Ray and told him that I was happy for Monica to be out of my life. My parents were elated, my friends were relieved, and I was on a high.

The next day, however, was different. The adrenalin had worn off and my whole system crashed. My heart shattered into a million pieces and my mind was going crazy thinking what the hell had I done. I had ruined the best thing I ever had, and I didn't know how to fix it.

I spent three days with my parents before returning to Hereford and, although outwardly I gave the impression that I was happy to be rid of Monica, I was in actuality planning how to get her back.

My mum had given me a stern warning of what would happen if I ever 'took her back'. She told me that my life would be hell and that Monica was dangerous, that Monica was sick, and I was not the one to help her.

It was cute the way my mum was protective, even at my age. My dad said nothing as usual, he didn't like to judge people like my mum did.

'Just be careful, son,' is all he said.

I decided against telling anyone that I wanted Monica back as I knew that everyone would disapprove, not just my parents, but my friends too. They didn't know her the way I did, they didn't love her the way I did. If only everyone could see the real Monica under all that bluster and fury, they would adore her as I did.

I knew that if I could only get her back then things would be different *this time*. I had been a man, I had thrown her out. Monica liked tough men, right? Surely this showed that I was tough, that I couldn't be messed with. Me throwing her out would change her crazy ways, it would make us stronger as a couple.

I didn't know whether she would come back, but I had a feeling she would, and if she did, then it was proof that it was meant to be.

On the train back home I smiled to myself, thinking once again of the life we could have together and the more I thought about it, the more I was sure she would come back.

I was so sure of this, that I didn't even bother chasing her, I planned to just *bump into her* and casually tell her to come back home. I would be a man about it, tell her to come back like it was up to her, like I couldn't care less if she did or not.

I staged the meeting and planned to *see her* as she walked home from work, but my plans went awry when I saw near Hereford station, just out of the blue.

I had to think on my feet, improvise. I had planned everything I was going to say, so all I needed was the attitude. Just walk up to her and be *a man* about it all.

'Monica,' I called.

Monica looked around and stopped when she saw me. Her face clouded over as she tried to look angry. How cute, I could have kissed her just for that.

'I need to talk,' I said, as I approached.

'I can't stop,' she said, 'I need to get home.'

Be a man. Be a man.

'Your home is with me,' I said – good start.

'Not anymore.'

Resistance? That was expected.

Be a man.

'I miss you,' I said. 'I don't want to live without you. It's horrible with you not there.

'You threw me out,' she said frowning. 'I can't forget that.'

'Don't throw this away,' I whined. 'I love you.' – oops!

'It doesn't matter,' she snapped back.

'I know you love me too.'

'It doesn't matter,' she said again.

My heart leapt. She *did* love me.

'We are strong,' I said. 'We can make this. I'll be better.'

'You said that before,' she said turning to leave.

'Please come back to me,' I pleaded.

She sighed. 'John, I'll have to think about it.' Then, 'I have to go. We'll talk later.'

'Okay,' I said eventually. 'Please don't throw this away.'

She said goodbye, and I watched her walk away, my heart filled with hope. It had not gone quite to plan, but, if the end result was her coming back then I would be happy.

We spoke that night on the phone, I would like to say that she was the one who called me, but alas I couldn't wait for that to happen.

Two days later I had gone to her new place, a dump of a shared house on the outskirts of town with dirty looking walls and sleazy residents that harassed her in the hallways. I had ordered a taxi and managed to load all her belongings in one go, and in just a few short hours Monica was once again ensconced in the flat.

There were ground rules of course. The most important on Monica's list was to get her name on the lease so that I could never throw her out again. The other rule was to give her space whenever she needed it.

I agreed to both.

My ground rule was simple – never leave me.

The next day I visited the estate agent from which I rented the flat. I asked about adding Monica's name to the lease and they told me that that would be fine if I paid the fees. I said I'd think about it.

When I got home, Monica was working on her NVQ for work.

'So?' She said asking about the lease.

I smiled. 'All done,' I lied.

'Baby, thank you,' she said jumping into my arms.

We're never going to split up again, I thought, *so we can save money, and it's only a little white lie.*

"I want you, I need you

I gotta be near you

Ooh, I got a strange kind of woman"

Deep Purple

After all this time of being together, I was still struggling to figure Monica out. What made her tick? How could I help her with her...problems? What could truly make her happy?

I knew that I was a part of the problem, a big part. I just wasn't...I didn't know, but I just wasn't...wasn't what she wanted? I knew that I had to try harder, to do what was expected of me. She wanted peace, so I would give her peace, okay, I'd tried that before, but I needed to try again.

The one thing that would really make her happy was a visit from her son, so I encouraged her to invite him, and when she had, and his visit was arranged, Monica was like a different person, she had a glow about her and if she was happy, I was happy.

He arrived on July 16th, the first-year anniversary of mine and Monica's first date. We went to London to collect him from Heathrow and I had spent a fortune arranging for him to have a great time there before heading home to Hereford.

He was to stay for three weeks and I had done my research. I had found out what he liked and filled the house with all his favourite things. He was a biscuit lover, so I bought a ton of biscuits; he had a sweet tooth, so I filled a giant jar with sweets of all kinds. I got in his favourite foods and planned to cook him fish and chips and a full English breakfast. His stay would be amazing.

But first, we had a week in London. I had bought tickets for Sea World and Madam Tussauds, tickets for the London Eye and the London Dungeons. I planned to take him to Camden Town Market and Covent Garden. Everything I could think of, I sorted it.

Monica was excited and her face, when she saw her son, meant the world to me. She hugged him and kissed him and clung to him as if he would disappear if she let go. It was magical to watch.

We booked into the hotel, his room next to mine and Monica's. As soon as we were alone Monica took off her clothes and lay on the bed and spread her legs.

'Fuck me,' she said.

When an attractive woman is that forward, then it is a gift for some, and admittedly, it was for me in the past, but now I looked at her and I could see in her eyes that what she wanted was pleasure for herself. Her craving had nothing to do with me or her love for me, it was selfish.

'I'm not in the mood,' I said.

She furrowed her brow, confused that I would want to turn down what she had to offer.

'Come on,' she said playfully. 'You know you want to.'

I smiled. 'We'll do it later,' I said softly. 'I'm sorry, I'm just not in the mood.'

I sat on the bed and she crawled over to me and grabbed my balls.

'You mean you can say *no* to this?' She said displaying her nakedness.

I gently took her hand from between my legs. 'Sorry, sweetheart,' I said.

She looked at me suspiciously for a few seconds, then, 'Fine,' she said scooting away.

I knew I had upset her, but the thought of sex without any emotion right now made me queasy.

The week in London didn't go quite as I had imagined. Her son was eighteen and the attention span of a goldfish. He is an amazing young man, he is smart and handsome and calm and level headed, but he moved at 200 miles an hour.

Everywhere that we went, he was bored in seconds. In Sea World he shot off in front and hardly looked at a thing; in the Dungeons he stood in the corner and I could see that he just wanted to get out of there asap; on the London Eye he looked out across London for a couple of minutes, then looked like he wanted to abseil off the damn thing just to get down.

He loved the Medieval night that we took him to because, Monica told me, there was food. He liked Camden Market for the shopping and Covent Garden for the same reason, but everything else seemed an inconvenience. Even in Madam Tussauds it was me and Monica that had all the fun.

When we got back to Hereford I laughed as I was witness to a typical teenage boy. He would stay in bed until two in the afternoon, he ate us out of house and home and watched goofy comedies on Netflix. It was a pleasure to have him stay, and I thought that I would be proud to be his step-father.

Monica was great for the most part, but even with her son a witness, she couldn't help herself. She would mostly wait until we were alone to call me names or heavily criticise me for something, but not all her remarks were hidden from view.

At breakfast one morning, when Monica was out, I spoke to her son about how much I loved his mother, but how it was difficult living with her.

He nodded a few times then said, 'I know. I can see how she speaks to you sometimes.'

'Yeah,' I said, 'it's humiliating sometimes.'

'I can see that,' he acknowledged.

When it was time for him to go back home to Romania, Monica insisted on taking him to the airport alone. I couldn't understand this as she had admitted that she wasn't confident in the *Big Smoke* on her own and, when she had to go to London one time to get a new ID card, she had asked me to call in sick just to go with her.

I text Monica later that day to ask if everything was alright, she text back to say that she was just getting on the train back home, so she would talk later. I checked the train times to see what time she was due back, but there was no train from London at the time she said. My suspicious mind got to work...she didn't want me to go, no such train? I text her to ask if she had gotten a lift with someone to the airport.

'No,' she text back. *'I'll see you soon.'*

I knew there and then that that was a lie.

"I hate myself for loving you
Can't break free from the things that you do
I want to walk but I run back to you
That's why, I hate myself for loving you"
Joan Jett & The Blackhearts

Things had changed since her son had gone back home, and not because she missed him, but because of some unexplained reason. There were no fights or cruel words, but atmospherically it had gotten colder, quieter, creepily so.

My mantra in my own head was *'why can't things ever be normal?'* That's all I wanted – normality.

Some days were better than others; some days we lived like a real live couple who spoke to each other civilly and enjoyed each other's company. We would venture out for a meal or the cinema or shopping and, my god, we actually had a great time. On other occasions it was living with a block of ice. This duality of existence was draining. I was speaking to Lizzie more, just to get things off my chest, and Lizzie being Lizzie, she listened without judgment or telling me to, 'shut the hell up.'

I was also throwing myself into work, and a lot of the shifts included sleep ins which alleviated the pressure to act a certain way in bed. Bed, which had increasingly become the place where complaints took place, with Monica telling me that I was disturbing her by *breathing*. On several occasions Monica got out of bed and went to sleep in the spare room because I breathed too hard or I cleared my throat or sniffed or dared to *move* in bed. Such were the complaints that I would lie still and virtually hold my breath so as not to disturb her, and tough luck if I had an itch or wanted to sniff or cough or even sigh; I would swallow down any urge to do anything that would make her mad.

By November the irritation within Monica had manifested itself into acts of mental torture.

'Are you on sleep-in at work tonight?' She asked.

'Yes, why?'

She was silent for a while, a sly smile creeping into the corner of her mouth.

'No reason. What time are you back home tomorrow?'

'Three thirty,' I said.

Another sly grin.

'Oh, okay.'

'Why do you want to know?' I asked, my suspicions aroused and also my paranoia.

'Because I need to know what time my lover has to leave,' she said.

Then she disappeared into the bathroom with her phone.

I did not know whether this was said to wind me up, or whether it was truth disguised as a joke, or whether something else was going on, whatever it was it had me anxious yet again.

I began to call her while I was at work, sometimes she'd answer, say she was tired and go, sometimes she wouldn't answer at all.

I was torn.

On the one hand, I was miserable in the relationship filled with regret of leaving Lizzie, on the other hand, my heart was breaking thinking of losing Monica. And then one day she called me at work. She told me that she didn't love me and that she didn't think she ever did. She told me that she thought it was best if we split up as she didn't think it was fair on me to live with someone who didn't have the same feelings as I had for her.

'I've tried to love you,' she said. 'I wanted so much to love you.'

'That's not true,' I told her. 'You said you wanted a child with me, that I was the only man you ever wanted, that you wanted to marry me. You don't say all those things if you don't love someone.'

'I know,' she said coldly, 'but it was all a lie. I really wanted to feel love for you, but I couldn't. You don't want to love me and me just keep trying do you?'

To my shame I said, 'Yes.'

It was like my common sense was being drowned out by stupid blind love. I knew that it was a moronic thing to say, I knew I didn't mean it, but I couldn't stop myself.

I rationalised that, if I gave it time, she would stop being stupid and just love me like she was supposed to, and, as the next couple of days passed that's what she did. But the cruelty of it all was taking its toll on me. I wasn't eating much at all, I wasn't sleeping, I was shaking, even while sitting, my knee bounced like crazy.

I was so happy when Christmas rolled around, because Monica loved Christmas and it brought out the best in her.

We went shopping for Christmas decorations and a tree and lights, I had never liked the whole Christmas thing, but if it made Monica happy then call me Daddy Christmas.

We laughed and laughed some more as we decorated the house and put up the tree. We threw on the tinsel and the fairy lights, and Monica hung chocolates and Christmas baubles, then we took photos of the tree and of each other – it was a wonderful time.

As I watched her work on the tree and listened to her laugh I glowed inside and as we made love that evening I allowed myself to think:

'Maybe 2017 will be our year.'

"I don't hear your knock upon my door
I don't have your lovin' anymore
Since you been gone I'm a-hurtin' inside
Well I want you baby by my side
Yeah I'm cryin'"

The Animals

Christmas Eve was our Christmas Day. I was working on Christmas Day, care is an all year-round job, so all our plans were moved to the day previous.

We got up early in the morning, our presents laid out for each other, well, her presents and my present, singular.

Monica opened hers first.

She had warned me not to, 'get me shit like last year.'

Apparently, women don't like books and CDs and DVDs, they prefer jewellery and pyjamas and underwear.

I had bought her a pair of pyjamas, a work-out mat and a large jewellery box containing a ring she'd seen, and a necklace. I bought her Marks and Spencer's underwear, which she loved, and a Calvin Klein watch, and for a joke present, I bought her a clit stimulator and a vibrator. She was delighted with all.

I opened my present excitedly, and I was jumping with joy before I had even unwrapped it fully. Several months back I had been to the doctors because I'd had trouble with my hearing. The doctor asked me about my history and concluded that I had hearing loss because of my passion for loud rock concerts. A recommendation was to wear headphones rather than ear buds to prevent further damage. Monica had taken this on board and had bought me a pair of Beats by Dr Dre wireless headphones.

I tore open the box and took out the headphones. Now, don't ask me why, but yet again, my *stupidity* brain cell was obviously in complete control.

'They're pink,' I said.

Monica frowned. 'Well, it said red on the box.'

'Look,' I said showing them to her, 'they're pink.'

'So, you don't want them?' She asked.

'It's Christmas Eve, HMV will be open today, can we exchange them?'

It was probably the most selfish thing I've ever said.

Even so, Monica and I went into Hereford and tried to exchange them for a different colour. HMV told me that Apple, who make Beats, had a policy not to exchange once the box is open.

I was furious. How stupid.

I should have stopped there, but I went on and on about how unfair the policy was and even went so far as to call Apple. Monica offered to buy me something else and give the headphones to her son, but I said no. For an hour I complained. Monica had spent £200 on a Christmas present and all I did was complain.

Monica was calm, but I guess disappointed because eventually she pulled on her coat and grabbed her bag and phone.

'Where are you going?' I asked.

'To Andreea's,' she said.

'What? Why?'

'Look,' she said calmly. 'All I wanted was a great Christmas Eve, to listen to music and eat some nice food and spend the day with you, but you spoiled that.'

I *had* spoiled the day, that was true, and I had blindly whined on and not truly understood the impact until Monica was standing in front of me, ready to leave. And the most impactful thing for me, was how calm she was.

'I'm sorry, Monica,' I said. 'I'll make the rest of the day all about us. We'll have a good time, I promise.'

'Too late,' Monica said. 'I'll see you later.'

'Please don't go,' I told her. 'I promise I won't be a dick for the rest of the day.'

Monica shook her head. 'I'll see you later.

As she walked out of the door I panicked. I don't know why, but my feelings were not about the fallout, they were about something else – her simply not being here.

She called an hour later to tell me that she would not be back that evening, which I knew, meant she wouldn't be back until Boxing Day as there were no trains on Christmas Day.

My mum called to wish me a merry Christmas and asked if I was okay.

'Me and Monica are back together,' I told her.

My mum snorted. 'I know, son, I'm not bloody stupid, I'm a mum.'

I told her what had happened and about Monica walking out.

'Well, what you did was selfish and stupid,' she said, 'I don't blame the girl. Wait 'til she comes back and then you better try making it up to her.'

My mum was right, I had been stupid and now I was alone at Christmas.

I spent the afternoon pacing the flat and trying without success to watch a movie to distract me. I couldn't eat or drink or sleep. I tried calling her a couple of times but there was no answer.

By the evening I was majorly down and by 11pm I decided to go out for a walk. I walked the streets, the cold biting at my skin, the frost making me slip and slide with every other step. What was going round inside my head was as cold as the night air, the little voice in my head reprimanding me over and over telling me how stupid I was, how pathetic, that I was a piece of shit.

As the distant bells struck midnight and Christmas Eve was replaced with Christmas day, my phone buzzed. It was a message from Monica.

'Wherever you are you can come back now, I'm home.'

I quickened my pace to get home, but that little voice in my head that had called me names was now talking again:

'Which Monica will you find at home?'

"I know I haven't treated you so right
But I won't lose your love without a fight
Hold on to the love we have together
Hold on don't you say goodbye"

Lionel Richie

When I got back home, Monica was lying on the bed in the foetal position, her eyes closed tight, the covers tucked beneath her chin.

I squatted down next to the bed and stroked her hair. At first, she didn't respond, but her eyes were closed too tight for her to be asleep.

Slowly she opened her eyes and when she breathed out I could smell the alcohol.

'I'm sorry, baby,' I began. 'I've been such an idiot. Are we okay?'

I continued to stroke her hair as she looked up at me, but did not speak. She looked sad, and as she let out a long sigh, I knew that something was wrong other than me.

'How did you get home?' I asked.

'Taxi,' she said.

I smiled trying to make light of it. 'That must have cost you a fortune, all to see me?'

'NO,' she said sharply. 'I couldn't stay at Andreea's'

'Why, did something happen?'

'She had a guy there,' she told me. 'He said nasty things to me.'

'Like what?' I said getting annoyed.

'Doesn't matter.'

'It does, I don't want anyone saying nasty things to you.'

She snorted an accusatory laugh. 'Whatever, it doesn't matter, but I told him to stop and he didn't, so I came home.'

'Okay, baby,' I said. 'Can I get you anything?'

'You can leave me alone,' she said.

'Are we okay though?' I asked.

Anger flared in Monica's eyes. 'I'm drunk and pissed off, leave me the fuck alone.'

I backed out of the room and stood in the kitchen for a few minutes. Yes, I'd done a stupid thing and spent a miserable Christmas Eve on my own and now my girlfriend has been verbally abused, but won't talk to me about it...

My head was in conflict here. I needed to give her space, that was clear, but there were so many emotions spinning around inside me that it was hard to cope. I knew I should be happy having my baby back, I needed to concentrate on that, but I started to shake.

I had choices, but I knew the choice of going into Monica would be a disastrous one, the choice of going for another walk would also be disastrous. So, I made a third choice, unwise still, but I needed to stop my shaking.

I had been tee-total for fourteen years, but tonight was not one for counting days. I took a bottle of Becks beer from the fridge, popped the cap and tossed it on the counter top. I took the beer into the lounge. The Christmas tree flashed in the corner, people were talking loudly as they passed my building on their way home from the pub, there was joy in their voices and I was jealous.

I raised the bottle, a salute to insanity. As the bottle touched my lips the door to the lounge opened sharply. Monica came in like a whirlwind and seeing the bottle in my hand, leapt at me. She tore the bottle from my grasp and threw it across the room.

'What do you think you're doing!' She shouted.

But I did not have time to answer. She began to scream wildly and ran at the tree. She tore down the tree, stamping on it, throwing pieces of it across the floor. She pulled a canvas from the wall and stamped on that too, snapping it into pieces – all the time screaming.

'Monica, stop,' I pleaded. 'Please, Monica.'

She did stop, but then she turned her anger on me. She ran at me, punching me in the head and neck, kicking my legs and trying to kick me in the balls. Her head whipped from side to side, the screaming was shrill and inhuman.

I backed away, my hands held up to protect my face too stunned to even beg her to stop.

She ran from the room, throwing a chair as she did so. I followed her as she ran into the bedroom picking up the jewellery box I had bought her that day and threw it to the floor. She went to the desk and picked up the printer. She raised it above her head and was about to throw it at me when I snatched it from her hands.

Monica began to growl and spit, she pulled at her own hair and started to scratch her neck and slap her own face.

I came up behind her and wrapped my arms around her, pinning her arms to her side.

'Calm, Monica, please,' I said in obvious panic. 'I love you, I love you, calm please. Ssshhhh.'

Monica continued to scream and writhe in my arms, her legs kicking wildly to get free. I held her tighter so that she would not damage herself or the flat any more.

Then she bit me.

She sunk her teeth into my hand so deep that she drew blood.

I sprang away from her and she dropped to the floor and her body whipped like a fish pulled out of the water. I knelt next to her and she started to throw punches. I pinned her hands down and when I spoke my voice was cracking, close to tears, not with upset but with pure concern.

Her face was ashen, her eyes black and wild, foam was forming at the corners of her mouth as she growled and hissed.

'Monica, sshhh, I love you, it's going to be okay. It's going to be okay.'

I couldn't understand what was wrong with her, but I knew that this was far beyond just anger now. This was some kind of seizure, some mental illness.

I begged and begged for her to stop. I said her name over and over, told her that I loved her, reassured her that everything would be okay.

It seemed like hours passed until she calmed, but was probably more like twenty minutes. When she relaxed, I slowly let go of her wrists and helped her up. I picked her up in my arms and carried her to bed. I lay her down and fetched her some water, encouraging her to drink until the glass was empty.

I tucked her into bed and sat with her until she drifted off to sleep.

I took photos of the trashed apartment and then spent a couple of hours clearing up the devastation that the latest episode had left behind.

At around 4am, I slipped into bed next to her and held her close. I wondered if I should have called 999 for the ambulance, or even the police. I wanted to help her, but I didn't want to hurt her. I thought that whatever this was I would see her through it. Whatever was wrong, I would be there for her.

We'd be okay, I was sure of it.

"Come on baby

You know you drive me up the wall

The way you make good

On all those nasty tricks you pull

Seems like we're making up

More than we're making love"

Aerosmith

Christmas morning was tense.

I tried talking to Monica about the previous evening, avoiding talking about the violence and concentrating instead on the seizure-like *attack* that she'd had. Although my dialogue came from a place of love and concern, Monica focused on the fact that I had nearly had a drink after fourteen years on the wagon. Each time she tried to change the subject, I dragged the conversation back on topic, only to have her avoid the discussion in favour of what she saw as my *faults*.

Eventually, upon my persistence to stay on point, she decided on a new tact and insisted that she couldn't remember what had happened.

I inadvertently rubbed the bite mark I had received during her *fit,* but I decided not to bring it up.

I told Monica that I was concerned and thought that she should see somebody. I told her that I was there for her, but I thought that she needed help from someone more qualified.

Monica's response went on a journey during our conversation. At first, she agreed she needed help, but was scared to see someone; this was probably the most honest Monica had been with me or herself about the way that she was. I reconfirmed my commitment to help her and told her repeatedly that I loved her.

Monica then moved from an admission to, *'I only need you.'* She didn't want to see anyone, she didn't *need* to see anyone, as long as I loved and supported her, then she'd be fine. I tried to bring her back to her original admission, telling her that there was nothing to be afraid of, that the way she had been was scary to witness and that she would end up hurting herself.

I began to see physical changes in Monica as we talked. Her body language grew fidgety and twitchy, then stiff and defensive. Her posture grew somewhat confrontational, her physiognomy grew strong with piercing eyes and squared jaw.

She moved on from wanting me to help, to blaming me. She said that I was trying to make her *look crazy*.

'You're saying I'm mentally ill, giving me a disorder, playing doctor.'

'You foamed at the mouth,' I told her. 'You twitched and growled and you say you can't remember any of it. You need help, Monica, I'm not saying you're mentally ill,' I lied.

The final stage in her metamorphosis was the defence via coldness. Her body language became loose and casual, she shrugged and shook her head a lot. She laughed, a snort without humour. She had used this laugh during many of our fights to humiliate me, a *I don't give a shit* laugh, icy and emotionless.

'You make me like that,' she said in conclusion. 'Without *you* I'd be fine. It's *you* who drives me fucking mad.' She poked herself hard in the temple with a stiff finger. 'You make me like this. All I need is peace, just leave me alone and I'll be okay.'

That afternoon, I went to work full of anxiety. The following few days were no less anxious. Monica was pure CO_2. If I tried to talk to her she would complain that I wasn't giving her peace. If I tried to hold her at night, she would take my hand and toss it to one side. She would greet me from work with a smile and tell me that she had used the vibrator on herself, but not want to make love with me. She began to lock the door when she had a shower and change in another room. Monica was shutting me out.

I used her laptop one afternoon and saw that the Facebook page was not hers but Gabe's, her ex. There is an argument to be made, that I should have respected her privacy, but why did she have his Facebook page on her computer?

I clicked on the messages and was faced with weeks of messages between them both. Gabe's messages were full of heart emojis and declarations of love. Monica did not reciprocate, but there were several messages setting up times and places to meet.

I confronted Monica about this.

'I set a trap for you,' she told me. 'I left that on my computer because I knew that you would spy on me. I can't trust you.'

Each time I tried to talk about her sneaking off to meet her ex, she would turn it around again and call me untrustworthy. Eventually, I found myself apologising for even daring to look at the messages.

She had found a game on the laptop too, a MMORPG (Massive Multiplayer Online Role-Playing

Game). She spent all her time playing it, a further excuse not to communicate with me. I came home one evening from work and she was sitting in bed playing the game talking to another player in Romanian.

'Who's that you're talking to?' I asked.

'Mind your own business,' she said.

Again, I told Monica of my unhappiness with this, and again I found myself apologising for questioning her.

Monica also took a trip to Romania for two weeks to her brother's wedding. I got along with her brother and liked her son, so I wanted to go, but Monica said no, making it clear that I would not be wanted.

Those two weeks were painful as hell. I volunteered to work eighty hours a week, just to occupy my mind. Monica hardly called or even text and when she did, it was to brag that she was having a great time without me.

When Monica returned it was much of the same, the cold shoulder, distancing herself, shutting me out. My emotions were quicksand and I was sinking into the quagmire of depression. I couldn't eat or sleep properly.

My heart broke each time she was cruel:

'I wish I never met you.'

'Don't touch me, you make my skin crawl.'

'I can't even bear to look at you.'

I couldn't believe how hateful she was and how that hate made me feel – belittled, humiliated, ashamed and, yes, fearful.

I had *no* confusion now about which Monica was waiting for me at home, I knew that it would be the 'hateful Monica'.

When my parents called I would tell them that I was fine, that me and Monica were happy and that, *'Monica says hi.'*

But I was far from fine, far from happy.

I felt so alone.

"All you wanna do is hold her
But she don't go for that
She has a hard time coming
When she can't hit back"

Matchbox Twenty

Arguments were rare, the forced isolation being the preferred method of torture, but when arguments did flare up, they crept up on me born from an innocuous comment, a look that I may have gotten wrong, my tone of voice that didn't sit well with Monica, and god help me if I was critical or dared to question what she was doing, even being *nice* could be deemed as wrong.

'It's freezing this morning, Monica, I'd wrap up warm.'

'Stop telling me what to do.'

'I'm just saying…'

'You're telling me what to do. You're trying to control me.'

I was also not allowed to complain about anything. I was not allowed to be upset or irritated or annoyed. My emotions were a prisoner within my own body, with no chance of parole.

I had begun to stutter when I talked to her, my brain panicking to find the right words so as not to offend or annoy.

I would fidget and pace while I spoke to her, the hyperactivity of anxiety, but even that drew her angry eye.

'Why are you pacing?' She would ask. 'You're getting on my nerves, stop it.'

She had given up sneaking around to meet Andreea or Gabe, now she openly went out, a smile slashed across her face like some psychotic Batman villain, pleased that her actions hurt me.

I began to see her as a monster, but still the thought of her leaving was *more* frightening. I was trapped by my own emotion, my inability to move on without her. I didn't know why I loved her or needed her in my life. I knew she was wrong for me on so many levels, especially for my emotional and mental health, but I could not leave.

There seemed only two ways to escape this suffering, her death or mine. Mine seemed the more plausible, it was in my hands after all, but did I have the guts to do it?

When we did argue, it was savage and brutal. Monica's verbal assaults were an oral exercise to find the most hurtful thing possible.

'I don't love you, I never loved you.'

'I'm going back to Gabe.'

And the worst –

'If I got pregnant with your baby I'd have an abortion.'

Monica was shouting, my brain numb.

'I fucking hate you,' she said. 'You've ruined my life. I'm so glad I never had your baby. I wish I'd never met you, people warned me, but I didn't listen. I fucking hate you.'

I stuttered something out, a mumbled retort with no power or substance.

She screamed and pulled her own hair, she struck herself twice in the chest.

'See what you make me do,' she said, getting in my face. 'I…hate…you.'

I stood there like some wax works doll, my replies were inaudible verbal dribbling's accompanied by sharp intakes of breath and the avoidance of eye contact.

She screamed in my face, an asylum sound that went through me.

She went into the kitchen and returned with a pair of scissors, my eyes widened, my heart began to beat hard against my ribcage.

'I'm going to cut up all my clothes,' she said, moving towards the wardrobe. 'I want to destroy everything, I hate everything.'

I moved quickly, fear as my motivation. I took the scissors from her and dropped them behind me.

'Don't, Monica,' I pleaded.

'Get out of my way,' she growled as I stood between her and the scissors. 'MOVE!'

I stayed where I was, too afraid of what might happen if I allowed her to get to the scissors.

Another scream, another pull of her own hair.

'I hate you,' she barked.

Then boom!

The punch came so quickly and struck the side of my head. I did not move, I was literally out of ideas.

Monica hit me again, a solid punch to my jaw. The punches then gained momentum. Monica began to pound on me, she hit me again and again and again and again. Blow after blow about my face and my chest and kicks to my legs. I stood and took it, my body and brain numbed and unable to take any action.

Then she planted a blow with perfect precision in my left temple. My head began to spin and my legs buckled from under me and I dropped to the floor. I could hear Monica yelling down at me through a filter of ringing in my ears.

'Faker,' she said. 'That didn't hurt you, get up...get up!!'

I stayed where I was, unable to get to my feet and also believing I was safer on the floor.

Monica continued to yell, telling me how much she hated me and how pathetic I was.

I waited, unmoving until she had finished. She stood over me for a few seconds, her body tensed with rage, and then she walked away. Moments later she was back and took her coat. She looked at me as if I were some strange and disgusting creature and then walked out of the apartment.

I sat on the edge of the bed, my hands gripped tight together to stop them from shaking and I breathed deeply to try and ease the pain in my chest.

I just kept hearing that scream and seeing flashes of her black-eyed rage, all that hate, the verbalised bile, the violence.

I took several moments to calm myself and picked up my phone. I searched the internet for the number I needed and dialled. It seemed to take forever for someone to answer, but eventually a soft voiced woman answered.

'Hello.'

'Hello,' I said. 'Victim Support? I'd like to speak to someone please.'

"Dying is easy

It's living that scares me to death"

Annie Lennox

There were no good times now, no rays of light, no love, no compassion; there was no Monica that I had met, *that girl* had long gone, and with her my smile, my joy, my reason for living. I felt as if I were at the bottom of a hole so deep and black and cold.

The Arctic like attitude from Monica was the only thing I knew now, and no matter how I tried to approach the problem I was rebuffed. I wandered through my days in a daze, unable to get my brain working and think logically. All I could do was wait for the meeting with Victim Support which was in a weeks' time.

In the meantime, they had suggested that I call the Men's Advice Line as this was the only helpline that they could think of that dealt with male victims of abuse. With the hundreds, maybe thousands of routes for abused women to go down, my choice was limited to this.

I called them while Monica was at work and spoke to a guy with a heavy, London accent. I told him a concise recent history of me and Monica. I told him of my pain and confusion and of my deep love for

Monica, even though she had subjected me to so much.

The man listened with a sympathetic ear and told me that my priority was to keep myself safe, that, if I could not leave, then I must keep her at arm's length, figuratively and literally. He told me that, no matter how much I love her, I would never be able to help or change her, that he couldn't tell me what I should do, but getting out of the relationship would be the wisest move.

He then asked if I had called the police.

'No,' I said. 'Should I?'

I know that it was something that played on Monica's mind. On two occasions during a fight, one of which ended in her punching me in the stomach, thigh and jaw, I had walked out of the flat just to get away. Monica had followed me to the top of the stairs.

'What are you going to do now,' She had shouted, 'go to the police?'

So clearly, she knew that she had been in the wrong and that it was reportable.

The advisor was thoughtful. 'You can call the police,' he said carefully, 'but be mindful that it may not go your way.'

'How so?' I asked.

'Well,' he began. 'You're a man, and I know that sounds bad, but I'm going to be honest with you here. If you report her for hitting you, the most, and I mean *most,* that you are going to get, is them talking to her.'

'Even when she attacked me like she did?' I said.

'Yes. If she counter accuses you, even if you did nothing, just the accusation could see you in a cell for 48 hours.'

I couldn't believe it. How could the law be so skewed in this day and age, the so-called, age of equality?

After the phone call, I felt a mixture of emotions. On the one hand, I felt better talking about it all, on the other, I felt just as trapped as before, if not more so. I know that Monica had accused me of rape and, even though that was not true, if she was to mention that to the police, there would be no benefit of the doubt, I would be taken for questioning…at least.

I had to hang on for the Victim Support meeting and see if they can give me more constructive help than the Men's Advice Line.

I couldn't believe that there were only two sources of help for male victims of abuse. I could only find a couple of books on the subject and only two movies. Only one of these has had any publicity – *Disclosure.* However, this film starring Michael Douglas and Demi Moore, was about sexual harassment, not domestic violence.

In the meantime, I was still living with a woman who was determined to make me suffer. I took the advice I had been given and backed off from Monica. I gave her space and kept away from her as much as possible. However, Monica had other ideas.

The *leaving her alone* policy was giving her what she wanted – peace, but it also gave me peace too and that was not on Monica's agenda. She began to pick on everything I did or said. She began to complain about the TV shows I watched or the music I listened to. Everything connected with me was *shit.*

I was not allowed to enjoy life at all. The only rest I got was working, and that was spoiled by her constant subliminal suggestion that she was cheating on me while I was on a sleep-in.

If I did 'answer back', then she used this as a perfect excuse to fly into a rage, however, each time she came at me, I held my hands out at arm's length and asked her to stay back.

She would ridicule me for this:

'Stay back,' she'd say in a childish voice. 'Don't come any closer. You are pathetic.'

I tried to stay calm, just focussing on the meeting that was coming up soon.

When the day came, I was relieved. I had no idea what they could possibly do, but I just needed to talk.

I left the flat in the morning. Monica was home, so peppered me with questions about where I was going.

'I'm just going for a walk,' I told her. 'I'll be back later.'

'Pity,' she said.

The meeting was held in a room at the community centre on the outskirts of town. The woman I was to meet was named Kim, and when I met her, she smiled a smile that instantly made me feel at ease.

Kim was in her fifties, she had long greying hair and kind eyes. When she spoke, her voice was soft and genuine and compassionate.

We sat for an hour and talked. I told her everything about myself and Monica, the good and the bad. Kim asked me questions and filled out a form that would give me a score to tell her, and me, the 'level of risk' I was at.

'If you reach a certain score,' she told me, 'I will have to inform the police.'

Because of this I downplayed some of my answers, the thought of my conversation with Men's Advice Line still fresh in my head and the warning about police involvement.

Kim, like the Men's Advice Line, told me that she could not tell me what to do, but I needed to get free of the relationship.

'Is your flat under both your names?' She asked.

'No,' I said, 'my name only.'

'Can you throw her out?' Kim asked.

I shook my head. 'I can't,' I said. 'She is a human being after all.'

Kim looked at me earnestly. 'Look, John, you told me that she has never used weapons and I'm telling you – yet.

' I know she is a human being, but you have to keep yourself safe. She's a woman and there's a lot of help out there, if she can't find a place to stay then there are shelters. She wouldn't be left on the street.'

I walked away from the meeting knowing that I couldn't take much more and that Kim was right, I *could* be in danger.

When I got home, Monica was playing her video game. I went into the living room and thought about what had been said and against all logical judgment I decided to try and get a dialogue going with Monica again.

I walked into the bedroom and asked Monica if we could talk.

'Do you really fucking call this leaving me alone?' She snarled.

'I don't like the way we are,' I tried to explain. 'Can we talk? This silence is no good.'

'I'm okay with it,' she said.

'Monica.'

'LEAVE...ME...ALONE!!'

'Why can't you be the Monica that I fell in love with?' I asked.

Monica stared at me with pure hatred. 'This is me,' she said, 'get over it.'

I walked out of the room and went into the small bedroom and shoved some socks and underwear into a bag and turned to leave.

Monica came into the room standing between me and the doorway.

'What are you doing?' She asked.

'I'm leaving,' I said.

'Where?'

'I don't know,' I admitted. 'I just need to get out.'

'You're not going anywhere,' she said. 'Don't be stupid.' There was no seductive tone this time around, this was a command.

I attempted to get passed her and she pushed me back and punched me in the face.

'I don't love you,' she said.

'Then leave,' I said. 'Get the fuck out and leave.'

'You always make me out to be the bad guy,' she said.

I felt nothing now, not love or hate or anger or compassion, I was emotionally numb.

'That's because you *are* the bad guy,' I said.

I went to walk around her again and again she pushed me back and again she hit me, this time a solid slap across the cheek.

I pushed her on to the bed and walked out of the room. Monica ran after me and punched me in the back of the head, I was so dazed I just kept on walking until I got to the bathroom, I went inside and closed and locked the door behind me.

Monica balled and shouted at me from the other side of the door. I waited her out, my back against the door, my head empty of thought, my body empty of feeling.

When I heard that she had gone quiet, I exited the bathroom.

'You need to leave,' I said calmly. 'Your name is not on the lease, you need to leave *my* flat.'

'I knew you lied,' she said, looking slightly concerned.

'Let's not talk about lies,' I said. 'When you went to London taking your son to the airport, I know it was Gabe who gave you a ride.'

'Yes, it was,' she admitted. 'I...I wanted to save money on the train fare so that I could give my son the money.'

I shook my head. 'You have to go,' I told her.

'You want me to leave now?'

I nodded. 'Yes. I'm sorry, but I can't take this anymore.'

I walked out of the bedroom and out of the apartment. Within 30 minutes I received a text.

'You can come back now, I've gone.'

"Now I've got that feeling once again
I can't explain you would not understand
This is not how I am
I have become comfortably numb"

Pink Floyd

I called my friend, Wayne, and told him that Monica had gone, gone for good this time.

'She is an evil bitch,' he told me. 'A real evil fucker, mate. You can't let her back this time. Don't dare let the bitch back.'

Wayne seemed to feel more emotion than I did. I didn't feel anything. I didn't feel sad or angry or depressed or relieved...nothing. It was as if that last slap she had given me turned off my brain, just flipped a switch turning off all the lights. I was dead inside.

I moved through the days like an extra from a George Romero movie, I had no pain, but no pleasure either. I buried myself in work, working every day I could, and mostly fifteen-hour days.

Kim from Victim Support was calling me every day. She was as concerned about my 'inability to feel' as she would have been if I was crying all the time. She suggested that I go to see the doctor and I took her advice.

Doctor Corbett was amazing. He did not rush me when I began to talk, he listened and was sympathetic and non-judgmental, he treated me no different than if it were an abused woman sitting in front of him. He asked me questions to judge my thought processes and my emotional state.

'Well, you are a brave young man,' he said. 'You have taken the first big step and most important step, talking about this, a lot of men would not talk about it or seek help.'

I did not consider myself *brave* in any way, I considered myself desperate for help.

By the time I left his office, he had referred me to *Let's Talk* for counselling and I had a handful of prescriptions – Sertraline and Amitriptyline which are antidepressants, and Propranolol which is a beta-blocker. I also left with a stern warning that going back to her could be dangerous.

Back at home I was making changes. I had called the charity shop and they had come to pick up and take away furniture that Monica had bought, the dining table, the dressing table, the desk. I replaced the flowery canvasses in the bedroom with black and white photos of Marlon Brando and Clint Eastwood, I bought myself a record player – something I would never be allowed to have while with Monica. I threw out the bedding and the throws on the sofa, I threw out the pots and pans, the plates and mugs, even the cutlery, everything that Monica had brought with her or bought since she had been in the flat was gone.

All this change made the flat more *mine,* but it was done with a cold detachment.

As the first week rolled by, my zombie-like nature had not gone away. The people I spoke to found me a distant disinterested John, people *blah blahed* at me complaining about their life and work and their kids and the weather…it was just noise to me, and boring noise at that. I snorted and hummed and ahhhed and basically, grunted my way through one-sided conversations, and with egos as they are, I don't even think that they noticed my 'other worldliness'.

Ten days after I had thrown Monica out, I was sitting at work, Jeremy Kyle talking to some half human idiot on the TV, when my phone buzzed. I pulled the phone from my pocket and found that I'd had a message – from Monica.

'Don't call me or start a conversation, just tell me if you're ok, yes or no.'

I stared at the screen for the longest time and then tossed my phone to one side. A half-hour later, my phone buzzed again.

'??'

I sighed and just typed, *'No.'*

Almost immediately my phone buzzed for a third time.

'Why? What's wrong?'

'What do you think?' I said.

'What's going on?' She asked.

I didn't answer for twenty minutes, undecided what to say, or if I should answer at all.

'I'm on three types of medication and I feel nothing,' I said. *'That okay? Now you know.'*

'Because of us?'

Now she was beginning to irritate me. *'Yes,'* I wrote.

'I don't want you to be taking pills,' she said. *'I want you to be okay. I care about you.'*

I read this and put my phone away. Monica caring about me did nothing to move me to an emotion of any sort, it was like reading a food packet, it meant that little.

The next day Monica text again:

'How are you?'

'Look, Monica,' I text, *'What do you want?'*

'I want to make sure that you're okay.'

'I'm fine, there, satisfied?'

'I don't want you taking pills,' she said.

'Tough,' I replied.

Again, I put my phone away and did not answer any more messages, didn't even look at them.

The next couple of days were streams of texts from Monica, some of which I answered, some of which I didn't. She kept telling me that she didn't want me on medication, that she was worried about me. When I didn't reply she would ask me why I wasn't answering or saying that *needed* to know that I was alright.

As the messages kept coming my emotions began to break through. I fought against them as soon as I was aware. I tried not to care, I really did, but she wouldn't stop texting, and something stopped me from blocking her, although I wanted to.

Eventually, Monica text, *'I want to see you.'*

My logical brain was screaming like a mental person to not agree to a meet. The words of Wayne and Doctor Corbett yelled at me not to meet her.

'Okay,' I text.

The next day I was in my kitchen, when I heard Monica come up the stairs. She came through the door, a shallow smile on her face.

She looked so beautiful.

'How have you been?' She said shyly.

'Okay,' I told her.

We sat in the living room and talked. She asked why my leg was bouncing as I sat on the sofa, I was unaware that it was – nerves?

She commented on the changes I made to the place and the small talk seemed to fade to looking at each other. After twenty minutes she got up to leave.

I walked her to the door when she turned.

'You take care,' she said.

She moved closer and at once we were kissing.

"Baby I don't want you, but I need you
Don't wanna kiss you, but I need to
You do me wrong now, my love is strong now
You've really got a hold on me"

Smokey Robinson

From the first moments our lips touched I was lost. We held each other tight, both of us getting lost in the kiss. We started pulling at each other's clothing as we moved towards the bedroom never breaking the kiss.

We made love with a passion that I hadn't felt for a long time. I had longed for this; my body had cried out for it during the period that Monica had shut me out. My brain forgot all about the pain and hurt I had gone through, the words of my friend, Wayne, and Doctor Corbett forgotten, thrown in the trash.

Monica sighed and groaned and called my name. She told me that she loved me and what I did to her over and over. She told me that she wanted me, needed me, that I was the only man she wanted.

When it was over I collapsed, exhausted physically and emotionally. My zombie-like state was now awash with new and exciting emotions.

I looked over to her and saw her looking at me. I brushed hair from her face and stared at her beauty. There seemed to be so much love in her eyes.

'I have to go,' she said at once.

'Don't leave,' I pleaded.

She laughed playfully. 'I have to, I wasn't…we weren't supposed to do this.' She leaned over and kissed me softly. 'I love you.'

For the next several days we text and talked, sometimes late into the night. Monica told me that she loved me and that she couldn't wait to be with me again. I would sometimes answer her straight away, but sometimes deliberately not answer for an hour or so, the casual approach.

Several days later she came to see me again, but this time there was no preamble, no chit chat, it was purely sexual. It was wild and hot, and she did things to me that blew my mind.

She said all the things I wanted to hear:

'I love you.'

'I can't think of being without you.'

'Give me a baby, I want your baby.'

She even giggled sweetly as she told me about her using the vibrator on herself.

'It's amazing, but I can't come without thinking about you,' she said. 'I scream your name when I come.'

This time she lingered a little longer, holding me close and telling me how amazing I was, and how she wanted to be my wife.'

When she had gone, I lay in bed thinking about how much I missed her and how, when she moved back into the apartment, how different it was going to be *this time*.

I called her every day for the next few days, telling her how I couldn't wait for her to move back in with me.

'I'll have to think about it,' she said.

'What's there to think about?' I asked her. 'Just come back, we belong together.'

'But you threw me out,' she said.

I laughed, trying to turn it into a joke. 'You threw me out of our first house, well, gave me two days to leave, even stevens, come back.'

'You threw me out twice,' she said solemnly.

'So, it's not about the throwing out?' I said, 'It's about who threw who out the most?'

'Yes,' she said.

I took a deep breath. 'Just come back,' I said to her. 'We can put your name on the lease, we can go down together and do it.'

'I don't know,' she said. 'That flat...I don't know, it has bad memories now.'

'We can find a new place,' I assured her. 'We can find one together, as a couple.'

'I do love you, John,' she said. 'Let's take it slow.'

'Okay,' I agreed. 'I love you so much, baby. I just want to be with you always.'

'And I want to be with you,' she said back.

The following night we talked again, and again the night after that. We arranged for her to come to my flat again, and I grew excited to see her – but she never came.

I called her and asked her why she never came.

'Sorry, I was really busy,' she said.

'That's fine,' I told her. 'Let's say Saturday?'

'Yeh, Saturday would be better.'

Saturday morning came around and Monica called to tell me that she could not make it, but she would definitely come on Tuesday and even stay over.

Tuesday came and still no Monica. The no shows were making me anxious, I would pace the flat, thoughts crashing in my head of why she would cancel again and again.

Our conversations on the phone were still love-birdish, with plans for the future which included a baby, Monica had brought up the dreams of a family several times.

At 8.30pm one March evening, we had been talking on the phone for nearly an hour.

'God, I love you,' I told her.

'I love you, baby,' she said.

'When are you coming back? I need you,' I said. 'I don't ever want to be without you.' I started to sing. 'Stuck on you, got a feeling down deep in my heart that I just can't lose.'

Monica started to laugh. 'You're a shit singer,' she said.

'Come back home and I promise I'll never sing again,' I laughed. 'Seriously, if we are to move forward, then we have to do something.'

'That's true,' she said. 'I gotta go. I love you, John.'

'I love you too, sweetie,' I said. 'Talk tomorrow.'

'Yes,' she said. 'I miss you.'

The next day I text, *'Good morning.'*

There was no reply.

I tried to be casual about it, but my heart and mind and spinning stomach, full of anxiety, weren't going to let me off that easy.

I tried texting her another couple of times and then I tried calling.

No answer.

Now my body was in full panic mode. I needed her to answer me, I needed to speak to her, to find out what was going on.

I called her another five times and each time it went through to her answer phone.

'I'm coming around to see you,' I text hoping that this would make her answer me.

I was right.

'Don't come here,' she text back.

'Then what's going on?' I asked her.

'I don't think we should see each other anymore.'

'Why?'

'I don't want to be with you anymore,' she text. *'Don't contact me again.'*

'You're seeing someone else aren't you?' I typed.

'Yes,' she said. *'Don't contact me again.'*

I love you I want you I need you I want to have your baby You're amazing You're the only one for me I love you I lo...baby baby baby I hate you you piece of shit arrrggghhhhh baby I love you I want to stab you in the eye look what you made me do lies lies lies baby I love you I'm seeing someone else everybody hates you you could do better Monica cut your hair fatty fatty I love the way you look where are you going don't contact me again I need you I'm seeing someone else if I was pregnant with your child I'd have an abortion I love you don't speak to me hold me leave me alone I can't come without thinking of you don't touch me you make my skin crawl baby baby I want to marry you I'm seeing someone else hahahahahaha I don't love you look what you made me do I miss you cunt I love the way you are babyyyyyy you're the only one I want I need you you ruined my life I love you nobody likes you I can't come without you spoiled brat hold me hold me I hate you kiss me fuck me I want to stab you in the eye I love you baby abortion leave me alone hold me skin crawl look what you made me do love piece of shit I love you I want to die

"We said our goodbyes, ah, the night before
Love was in your eyes, ah, the night before
Now today I find you have changed your mind
Treat me like you did the night before"

The Beatles

Will somebody please stop this?

Will someone please take away this pain?

Will someone please shut off my brain?

Please

Please

I was light headed, disorientated. I tried to control it, I really did. I wanted my zombie-self back. I needed not to feel, needed not to think. I tried to call her, but she didn't answer, text her, but she did not reply.

Why so much pain?

I felt broken, like someone had taken a hammer to my insides. My chest hurt like a bitch and I found it hard to breathe. The weight of the stress and anxiety was bearing down on me, my back, shoulders and neck ached, my throat constricted, my mouth dry, and my head spun, memories spinning, words and images pumped emotions through my veins like an overdose.

I sent her a message to say I was coming to see her knowing that this ensured a response. Within a minute the phone rang.

Monica's voice was calm and cold.

'Go home, John,' she said, without preamble.

'Why are you doing this, Monica?' I asked.

'I just don't think we should see each other anymore,' she said offhandedly.

'Why? Who is this other guy?'

'Just someone,' she said.

'It's baldy bastard isn't it?'

'Yes,' she said directly.

'I fucking knew it,' I said, trying to control my emotions.

'No, I'm not seeing anyone,' she told me. 'It's his twin brother.' She sighed. 'No one.'

My head was exploding. What the hell was she talking about? Yes. No. Twin brother?

'You bitch!' I screamed.

'I think you should calm down,' she told me coolly.

I continued to rant at her trying to get some sort of emotion to reflect on the other end of the phone, but she had won. She didn't have to raise her voice, get upset, none of that, she had broken me, I was sure that was her aim. Those two days of love making, those words that she used to win me over again, to fool me into loving her again, had all been to regain control after I had taken that from her by throwing her out.

I put down the phone and fell onto the bed. I curled up into a tight ball and hugged myself. I felt as if I was in that pit again, deep and dark but this time slowly filling with water.

I did not know what to do. I tried calling my parents and then Wayne, but I found no comfort in their condemnation of Monica.

I tried calling Lizzie, but she was very sparse in what she said and what she did say was, 'Take care of yourself, you're better off without her.'

I don't know what I expected from the calls, someone to say a magic word that would end all my hurt, but no one could do that.

I spent the next few days in agony. I would just spend my time either working, holding in all the emotion, or lying in bed trembling unable to move or eat. I popped pills like they were candy and I had even been to the doctors and was prescribed sleeping pills which sent me off to La La Land for a nice fifteen hours.

Kim of Victim Support was calling every other day. I would talk to her in a fairly incoherent way, just verbal riffs about how I felt, how Monica had done this too me, how I still loved her; and through it all Kim just listened with a sympathetic ear but gave little advice. What could she say? One thing that she did say that stuck with me after the phone call was, had I spoken to the police about the violence? My friend, Wayne, had said the same thing, but I had not taken it seriously. Now I did, especially as I had photographic evidence of my flat destroyed by Monica and the bite mark on my hand inflicted on me by her on Christmas Day morning. I also had an eleven-minute recording of her ranting at me and humiliating me.

I called Men's Advice Line again to get some perspective on everything, but this conversation was very unlike the first conversation I'd had. Instead of a guy who was all about active listening and empathy, I got a man who didn't really know how to respond.

I explained to him what had gone on and told him that I was thinking of going to the police. I acknowledged that there may be a counter claim of domestic violence by Monica, but I was the one with the photos and recording.

'Yeah, might be ok,' he said with a heavy cold. 'I can't tell you to do it or not to do it.'

I listened as he breathed heavily and snorted down the phone.

'You're out of the relationship now,' he continued. 'That's good.'

'She also works in care,' I told him. 'Do you think that's dangerous as I've seen her change on a dime from nice to out of control?'

He coughed and sputtered and breathed like an asthmatic Darth Vader. 'Dunno,' he said.

I ended the call more frustrated than when I'd made it and thought, *This is the only help for men out there?*

Perhaps I was being too harsh, perhaps I just got a poor advisor or an advisor on a bad day. Nevertheless, I still had a decision to make, do I go to the police and make a complaint or not?

Where was the real help for men? Newspapers, magazines, TV shows, celebrity interviews, they were filled with stories of evil men who beat up women and the charts were filled with songs of female empowerment, but there was little to no mention, of the evil that women do.

So, what could I do?

Who could help me?

On May 12th, 2017 at 7.30am, I walked into the station of the West Mercia police.

"Sometimes these cuts are so much

Deeper than they seem

You'd rather cover up

I'd rather let them bleed.."

Maroon 5

The discussion was held in *interview room 1*, a room straight out of some dingy cop show sans the two-way mirror. The room was dimly lit, bare, with peeling painted brick walls, a recording device sat in the corner, a metal table sat in the middle of the room with a chair either side; the chair that I sat in was screwed to the floor, it was cold and uncomfortable. A camera looked down on me.

The police officer sitting across from me was a stern-faced woman whose voice had no inflection that suggested she was human.

I had spoken to her on the phone once before this meeting and I could tell then, that this was just a thing she had to do. She had shown not one iota of understanding on the phone and I could see here, that I would have to fight hard to get my case across.

She asked me to explain why I was there, so I told her the story of my relationship with Monica, the fights, the humiliation, the verbal abuse, the emotional abuse, the psychological abuse and, of course, the violence.

She listened to everything I had to say, only stopping me now and then to qualify something I had said. She made scant notes and nodded in the places that she thought she should.

When I had finished she said, 'Well, I can't do anything about the emotional abuse and stuff as there is no proof, and it would be impossible to prove.'

'Wait,' I said interrupting her. 'Theresa May has just introduced a law making emotional and psychological abuse a part of domestic abuse. This is the law, I'm not wrong on that, right?'

She shrugged and sat back in her chair and looked at me. 'What the government says and what we can prove is totally different,' she said. 'We can only go on physical evidence, something we can investigate, we can't investigate emotional abuse.'

This was stupid, and I told her so. 'But it's the law. You represent the law. Surely you…'

'Mr. James,' she interrupted me now. 'We can't prove anything. I'm sorry if this happened, but there's nothing we can do without evidence.'

'Then why have the damn law?' I asked getting upset.

'I know it must be hard.'

'What about medical evidence?' I said. 'I have doctors records and medication, I've been referred for counselling.'

'That won't stand up,' she said. 'I'm sorry but we only go after things where we think we have a good chance at prosecuting.'

I was frustrated. 'What use is this law then?' I asked impatiently. 'What is it, a governmental soundbite?'

Again, she shrugged. 'I'm afraid it could be.'

'What about the physical violence?' I asked. 'That's something you can prosecute. I have photos of my home smashed up and a bite mark on my hand.'

She sighed. 'Can I ask, Mr James, why did you not come to us before?'

I ran my fingers through my hair, tears crept into the corners of my eyes and my throat was so tight I found it difficult to talk.

'It…it's not as simple as just…just coming to you at any time,' I told her. 'You need to understand abuse, I…love her.'

'But you don't now?'

'Yes, of course I do,' I said.

'I'm just wondering,' she said. 'People might think, because you have finished now, because you have broken up, that this is payback.'

I couldn't believe what I was hearing. I didn't know that the police focussed on gossip, on what people's unknowledgeable opinions were.

'It's not payback,' I said my voice tinged with anger. 'I was abused, hit, slapped, bit and all the things that apparently you can't do anything about.'

She was silent for a few seconds, then, 'Can you email me the photo of the bite mark?'

'I can send you them all,' I said. 'I can send you the photos of my flat smashed up.'

'When was that done?' She asked.

'One on Christmas Day,' I said. 'The other was last year some time.'

She sighed again. I got the feeling that she just wanted me to disappear, she seemed irritated for having to listen to me. There was no sense of empathy or compassion.

'Well,' she said tapping her pen against her teeth. 'The earlier time it happened we can't do anything as it happened too long ago, and...'

'But people bring cases years after an event,' I said stopping her. 'I've seen it on TV.'

'I'm sorry, we can't do it,' she said.

I bowed my head, my options for justice were disappearing by the second. 'And the Christmas Day violence.'

She coughed nervously. 'The things she broke, were they yours or hers or belong to you both?'

'What difference does...they were ours, okay. I don't see...'

She was shaking her head. 'If they belonged to both of you, if she was partial owner, then she had the right to break them.'

'This is ridiculous,' I said, furious. 'What is the use of me being here.'

'Mr James, if we can be calm.'

'This woman has torn my life to pieces,' I said. 'She has attacked me and smashed up my flat twice. If I had done that to her, then I would be arrested.'

'Sir, I can assure you that there is no difference in how we treat men or women,' she said. 'Email me the bite you received, and we'll talk to Monica.'

Tears rolled down my face, my fists clenched tight trying to hold in the frustration, the stress, the sense of injustice.

'I know it's hard,' she said. 'I'll call you in a couple of days when I've spoken to Monica.'

I got up from my seat and shuffled towards the door.

'I think it would be best to see your doctor,' she said to me.

See my doctor? She hadn't listened to a word I'd said.

"I can't see the point in another day
When nobody listens to a word I say
You can call it lack of confidence
But to carry on living doesn't make much sense
…I can't stand losing you"

The Police

I waited and waited, but the police did not get back to me. A week rolled by and I was getting impatient. My days and nights had not improved, I was still working and then going home and collapsing into bed, blindly watching YouTube as my attention span could not last longer than a couple of minutes. I was swallowing medication like there was no tomorrow, feeling little to no affect, but scared not to take them. I would either not eat or eat piles of food that could just be shoved into the oven and consumed quickly, so I could go back to bed. I ate crisps and chocolate so that I wouldn't have to cook, I never showered on my days off and I would hold my bladder until near bursting because I didn't want to get up for the trip to the bathroom.

After a week I called 101, the police inquiry line, and made a complaint that I had not heard about my case. I told them that I had emailed the officer and received no reply – they said they would help.

Twenty-four hours later I received an email from the police officer I had seen, telling me that she had been busy and not spoken to Monica yet. I wondered if there would have been a delay if I had been a female, I bet not.

Another four days passed, and I called the station to check on the progress, or lack thereof. The officer seemed irritated again when she came on the phone.

'Mr James,' she said, sternly. 'I have spoken to Monica and she admits that you fought but that *both* of you were physical.'

'That's a lie,' I said. 'The only way I was physical was trying to hold her because she was smashing the place up.'

'Well,' she said, 'that can't be proven either way. There are no witnesses so it's your word against hers.'

'And you're taking her word over mine, obviously,' I said.

She was silent for a few seconds, then, 'I'm not taking anyone's side, sir, I just can't prove anything one way or the other.'

'But what about the bite mark?' I asked. 'There is photographic evidence of that.'

'She said you'd bitten yourself,' she said.

I was stunned, one, at what Monica had said and, two, that the police were stupid enough to believe her. 'Why would I bite myself?' I asked. 'That's just stupid.'

'But we can't prove any different, sir.'

'You can,' I informed her. 'You can get experts to look at the photo and examine our bite radius.'

'I'm sorry, sir,' she said with a finality.

'So, you're not going to do a damn thing?'

'I'm sorry, sir,' she said again.

I put down the phone.

Monica had gotten away with it all. The police were not interested, and I believed that there would have been a different response if Monica had complained about me.

I was close to tears now, every time that I was alone. I had started to pull my own hair and bite my fingers until I could not stand the pain any longer. I would stand at the side of the road willing myself to walk into traffic, or stand staring down at the knife drawer wanting to cut myself to pieces, but something inside was stopping me.

I started to have flashbacks too. It wasn't like in the movies, this was more surreal. I would walk into a room and it was like I was walking in on an already existing argument. I would see Monica, her face twisted, her black eyes big and exaggerated, her hands were usually claw like. I would see myself too sometimes, sometimes shouting, sometimes quiet and still. The flashbacks would last between a split second and ten seconds or more.

I would hear noises and become very jumpy, see things, shapes, mostly in the dark. On more than one occasion, I heard someone clearly say my name. It was disorientating and frightening.

A week later I received a phone call from a quiet spoken young man who told me that he was from Let's Talk and he wanted to offer me some telephone counselling. I agreed, and we talked for an hour. During this time, he asked me a set of pre-written questions with the aim of examining my mental state. The conclusion was that I was suffering from PTS (Post Traumatic Stress). He recommended that I see someone in person straight away, but explained that straight away in referral terms, meant months.

In the meantime, I was getting worse, emotionally, physically and definitely mentally. I sent a message to Monica's place of work including the photos of my smashed-up place and a warning of what she was capable of. This was because I truly felt that she could harm someone if she lost her temper, myself and others had seen her lose her shit at the care home we worked in together which had worried one of the team leaders so much he had asked me to 'Have a word', something I wasn't willing to do. I will admit, however, I needed some kind of justice and, although my concern for the people she supported was genuine, the justice element was a part of my reporting her.

I also text Monica and told her that all her belongings that still remained, were in the garage, to which she replied:

'Be there Tuesday.'

I got back from work on Tuesday and the belongings were still there. Wednesday, Thursday, Friday, still there. Even though they were not in my way it began to irritate me. I tried to call her to tell her to pick them up, but each time I did, I had to put down the phone because I could not bring myself to talk to her. I tried three or four times, but I only reached the point of an answer, once.

'Hello,' she said.

My mouth opened but wouldn't work, not a word would come out, so I put down the phone and screamed into my pillow.

I wondered if I would ever get over this, ever be normal. My body was constantly racked with pain, my mind a constant cocktail of self-hate, hate for Monica, love for Monica, and hallucinations that I could not stop even by closing my eyes.

Then the hole got deeper. I received a phone call from the police asking me to go in to see them.

'Why?' I asked.

'We've had a complaint,' the officer told me. 'Monica has reported you for harassment.'

"I see a red door and I want it painted black
No colours anymore I want them to turn black"

The Rolling Stones

The officer that I met at the station this time was even sterner looking than the first one. Her black hair pulled back harshly, and her young face set in a *don't fuck with me* stylee.

'Take a seat, Mr James,' she said.

I sat in the screwed down chair wondering what had been said.

'Before we start,' she told me, 'I must inform you that I will be recording this conversation, do you understand?'

I nodded, a frown painted across my forehead.

'I must tell you that you are not at liberty to say anything, but anything you do say may be taken down and used in evidence against you should this go to court.'

'What's going on here?' I asked confused.

'Do you understand?'

'Yes, but what the…'

'Monica has informed us that you have been harassing her. Did you send photos to her work and a message saying she abused you?'

'Yes,' I said. 'I am concerned that she could lose her temper and that she might harm someone. I've seen her lose her temper at work before, but I never thought anything of it, but then how she was with *me*, well...'

The officer stared at me for a few seconds before speaking. 'Well, Monica has told her boss that you are upset because you split up.'

'Well, it has nothing to do with revenge,' I said. 'Do you think that a person like her should be around vulnerable people?'

The officer looked at me as if I'd just killed her cat. 'We have spoken to Monica about your claims and nothing could be proven.'

'What about the photo of the bite?' I said, with desperation. 'I gave you a photo of that and that is proof.'

'We spoke to Monica about that,' she said. 'She said that she bit you in self-defence because you were on top of her.'

'This is just ridiculous,' I said.

'Did you call Monica and not answer her?' The officer asked.

'Sorry?'

She pulled out a piece of paper and read out some dates. 'These are the dates that Monica says that she received calls from you and you didn't answer her. We can check your phone if you like.'

'Yes,' I said. 'I called her to come and pick up her stuff, but I hadn't the heart to speak to her.'

'Well, Monica told us that she was too scared of you to pick up her things,' the officer said.

I was in shock, I couldn't believe this was happening. 'It's me who was afraid,' I told her, 'not her afraid of me.'

The officer sighed and shuffled the papers in front of her. 'I will have to go and talk to my boss,' she said. 'I need advice on what should be done.'

'What do you mean, done?' I asked.

'Well, this is serious, Mr James,' she said. 'It's clearly harassment, so I need to know if we give you a caution or not.'

'Sorry,' I said. 'If you give me a caution? So, this could give me a record?'

'Yes,' she said coldly.

The officer walked out of the room and I felt my insides cave in. Monica had hit me, bit me, tore my life to the ground and *I* am the one being threatened by police.

The officer came back into the room and handed me a sheet of paper.

'This tells you of the complaint,' she said. 'There will be no caution today, but you must not harass Monica again.'

I was furious. I stood up and screwed up the paper she had given me.

'This would never have happened if I was a woman,' I said. 'You're blaming the wrong person here.'

'I'm sorry you feel that way, Mr James. Shall I show you out?'

As I walked back to my flat I was a ball of anger and fear, fear of what could have been, fear of the what will be. I thought of hurting Monica in the physical sense, of making her suffer, making her pay for the pain she had put me through and was still putting me through.

Not even the police took me seriously, bending themselves into pretzel shapes so as not to do anything, yet I knew if I would have been a woman then action would have been taken. What was the point of law enforcement if the law wasn't going to be enforced? I even realised that Monica had changed her story about the bite mark, first it had been self-inflicted and then she had bitten me in self-defence, but the police had not picked up on her lie.

When I got home I paced my flat, my fury building, my hatred reaching fever pitch. I sat on the edge of the bed and punched myself in my own face. Pain shot through my jaw, but my anger was not satisfied with that. I hit myself again, and again. Each punch was more painful than the last, as I drove my fists into my jaw and my temples and rapped my knuckles hard on the top of my head. When I stopped I buried my face in my hands. I tried to cry, to let out what it was I was feeling, but nothing came, not a single tear.

I slipped off the edge of the bed onto my knees.

'Make it stop,' I whispered. 'Somebody, please make it stop.'

"I like the kick in the face
And the things you do to me
I love the way that it hurts
I don't miss you, I miss the misery"

Halestorm

Victim Support were calling me once a week, but I was lying to them now, telling them what I thought they wanted to hear, or maybe how I *wanted* to be. I said I was fine, getting stronger, coming to terms…but with what? I didn't even know what my own reality was.

The flashbacks had increased, so much so, that I actually feared them, tentatively walking into the bedroom, half expecting Monica to be there shouting at me. I could not watch the TV without hearing the name Monica, I was locking my door at night and putting the chain across and still there were noises that were either inside my flat or inside my head, strange hollow sounding noises that sounded like footsteps.

The nightmares came every few nights, dreams of Monica stabbing me, dreams of people surrounding me and screaming at me incoherently, dreams of me falling down the stairs.

And amidst all this, was my self-punishment. When things got too much emotionally, which was all the time, I would sit on my bed and punch myself in the face. I was careful not to give myself a black eye,

I was not looking for sympathy, I was looking for some kind of release, like people who cut themselves in hidden places, it's not about public display, it's about feeling something other than the emotional torture that's going on inside.

I would hammer my fists into my knees until I could not feel my legs, I would slam my hand in a drawer or kick a table leg with no shoes on, I would bite the inside of my lips and cheeks until I could taste blood. Sometimes the hurting would be purposeful, the punching myself in the head was mostly me sitting down to do just that, but sometimes it would be spontaneous, I would have hurt myself before I even had time to think about it.

I never cried, though I did try, I felt I needed the release of tears, but that manifestation of my sadness would not come, my only release was self-harm.

I did plan to harm Monica, however, all the time. I imagined her death at my hand on many occasions, but I thought how ironic it would be for me to take her life and then be locked up for the rest of mine – she would win again.

Days, weeks, months rolled by. I tried everything to stop the terrible agony I was in, I tried meditation and Qi Gong, I even turned to Buddhism, but nothing helped.

I started to write the story of my relationship called *Woman of Fury*, a hateful piece of work full of self-pity and exaggerated battles between me and Monica. I went onto Facebook and Instagram and tore Monica to pieces in my posts.

My friend, Wayne, who had been friends with both of me and Monica, had liked a few photos of Monica on Instagram after we had broken up. I sent him a message slating him for doing this, suggesting that he was *my* friend, so had no right to like anything of hers.

Wayne messaged me. *'John, you have to stop this. Me liking her photos has nothing to do with anything. You have to pull yourself together, because people will turn against you and, if the bitch decides to go to the police again, you could find yourself in trouble.'*

I wanted to shout at Wayne, ask him what the fuck I should do then, she has a life and I have nothing but nightmares.

So, I came away from Facebook for a while and continued with hitting myself for relief. Each day, the hole got deeper and deeper and blacker and blacker. There seemed no way out and suicide became an obsession. I would think about it all the time, too afraid to do anything about it. I spent hours willing myself to take that final step, but I just didn't have the guts.

In mid-August I sat in my room, I had just hit myself so hard in the temple that my vision blurred, when I snatched up the charging cable to my phone. I wrapped the cable around my neck and pulled with both hands cutting off my air supply. I pulled tighter, and the tighter I pulled, the more relaxed I became about actually dying. I saw the faces of Monica and my mother and Wayne and my friends Tara and Ray. The room began to swim, colours fading and running into a mass of grey, and still I pulled.

I passed out.

I don't know how long I had been out, maybe a few seconds, maybe hours, I didn't know, but when my eyes opened, I hated myself for not being successful and hated myself because I knew I would never be able to bring myself to finish the job.

I was a loser in every way.

"When I die, fuck it, I wanna go to hell

Cause I'm a piece of shit

it ain't hard to fuckin' tell"

The Notorious B.I.G

'I'm a piece of shit. I'm a piece of shit.'

Each time I uttered the phrase, I punctuated it with a punch, a pinch, a bite, a twist of the skin. This was a daily activity now, several times a day. I didn't tell anyone about it because I was ashamed of what I was doing, ashamed of how I felt.

It was early September 2017 and I had been hurting myself for months. I would look in the mirror and all I could see was an arsehole, a piece of shit, not worthy of love or even anyone's attention. I lied to my parents and my friends and my work colleagues, no one could know about how pathetic I had become.

The only person that I had told even a fraction of this to, was my GP, Emma. Emma had worked with abuse and mental health issues before, and she was so great. Like Doctor Corbett, she was non-judgmental and empathetic, she did not see me in a negative light, because I did what I did, but she tried to encourage me *not* to do it, but self-punishment was the only way I could find to release the tension that the pain created.

The one positive step I had taken, was to book myself a holiday in November, five days in India and then five days in Nepal. I needed to get away, to try and find some kind of answer to this…this…*whatever it was* that was happening to me.

On the evening of September 10th, 2017, I was working when my phone rang. I answered, and it was my mum.

'John, you need to get home as soon as you can,' she said. 'Your dad is in hospital and I think you should get here.

I began to panic as my dad had suffered with illness over the years and his second home was the hospital, but he had always pulled through. He had pulled through repeated bouts of bowel cancer, he had diabetes, angina, leukaemia; I asked him once if he was collecting diseases because he had that much wrong with him.

'When did he go in?' I asked.

'Three weeks ago,' my mum said. 'I'm so sorry I didn't tell you, but I know you had problems of your own. I should have told you, I'm sorry.'

'That's the least of my worries now, mum, I am at work now. I can come tomorrow as I'm on sleep in at work today, is that okay?'

'Yes,' she said. 'Just come when you can.'

Three hours later at 8pm my phone rang again.

'Hi, son, are you coming tomorrow?' She asked trying to sound calm and failing.

'Yes, I told you I'll be there asap.'

My mum told me that my brother and sister were at the hospital and that the doctors had said that there was nothing they could do for him, that he would not survive.

My heart broke.

My relationship with my mother had not always been great, we had fought constantly when I was a kid and only in the last few years had we bonded, basically because as my mum said:

'We're too damn old to fight.'

However, although I did not have anything in common with my dad, I looked up to him. My dad was a hero to me. He was loving and caring and never had a bad word to say about anyone. He was generous and funny and loved my mum like crazy.

In the last twenty years or more he had battled ill health and always come out the winner. With a positive attitude and sense of humour, he brushed aside his complaints with a smile. When he was told that he had cancer, his first reaction was not fear or self-pity but:

'Can my kids get it?'

Selfless.

In the past year he had lost that humour slowly and gained a more cynical outlook, believing that if he went into hospital that he would never come out again, and, even though there had been many visits to the hospital, and they had always resulted in a return, it looked as if he was going to be right this time.

'I have a bad feeling that I will never see him again,' I told my mum.

'Don't worry, son,' she said. 'You'll see him, nothing will happen tonight.'

At 11pm my phone rang again.

'Your dad has passed away,' my mum told me.

My trip to Stoke for my dad's funeral was one of the worst experiences of my life. The day after I arrived, we went to see my dad's body in the morgue. I had not cried for months, no matter how much I wanted to, instead I had turned to other means of getting a release. However, when I walked into the morgue and saw my father's body, my hero's body lying on the slab, his face sunken, his mouth open, his skin pale and cold, I cried – my god I cried.

My brother comforted me as I was uncontrollable in my grief, but my brother had no idea of the pain that was already in me, the pain that had been bottled up for months, begging to be released.

I cried so much I was bent double, and my brother supported me to a seat where I sobbed mostly for the loss of my dad, but partly for my own inner salvation.

Lizzie came to Stoke for the funeral, she was amazing in her support for me and my family. I cried at the funeral until there was not a tear left inside me.

When I returned to Hereford I returned to news that I was to begin therapy with Let's Talk, a part of me was relieved to be receiving help, yet another part of me was scared:

What would I be without this pain?

Something inside wanted and needed the hurt, the hurt was me, I *was* the hurt.

"I hate everything about you

Why do I love you?"

Three Days Grace

The counselling session was held in a small room with sterile white walls and bland pale blue chairs that sat across from one another.

The counsellor was a young woman that looked like a toned down new age therapist with patterned leggings and a cardigan. She was nice, a pleasant smile and softly spoken, she made you feel calm, which was good, because I was kind of nervous of what to expect.

'Hi, John, thanks for coming,' she said, as we took our seats. 'Today will be an introduction and a chance to get to know a bit about why you're here. Is that okay?'

I nodded. 'Yes,' I said quietly.

I had filled out a questionnaire online before going to the session, so we ran through that together. The questions aimed to rate my pleasure in doing things, my feelings of depression, my sleep patterns, my appetite and my feelings about myself.

My scores were mostly high as my PTS had affected my life as a whole, not just one aspect. My self-hatred had become a part of my make-up, no matter how ashamed I may have felt about it.

My counsellor explained to me that there were a couple of ways that she could help me, there was CBT (Cognitive Behaviour Therapy) or EMDR therapy (Eye Movement Desensitisation and Reprocessing). Many years back, I had seen a therapist to help me with panic attacks that I was having, I was scared of dying, well, not dying exactly, but not existing; the thought of dying and that being the end with no afterlife, caused great problems and I suffered overwhelming panic attacks, including chest pains and prolonged bouts of fear that would bring me to tears. For this I was treated with CBT which is, in essence, focussing on changing my thinking to alter my behaviour – it didn't work.

I explained that, on seeing my GP, she had told me about EMDR therapy and I was willing to give that a try. A second session was arranged for the following week.

In the meantime, I was trying everything not to hurt myself, but the temptation was hard to fight. I would hug myself as tight as I could, sit on my hands, clap my hands or just go out in public, anything to try and stop myself pummelling my own head. If the desire to hit myself got too much I would try and hit my knees or punch myself in the shoulder rather than my head or face.

The second therapy session rolled around quickly, and I found myself sitting face to face with the therapist, feeling very vulnerable.

After the initial introductions, she told me a little about what she was going to do.

'When we sleep,' she began, 'we reach a state called REM, which is Rapid Eye Movement. Here, our eyes go side to side and in this state, our brain is sorting through our day and making sense of it all, processing it all, and filing the memories and information away. The problem with your memories of Monica, is that they have not been processed and filed away, therefore they are just hanging around in your brain and that is why you get flashbacks, your brain still sees the memories as real, so you 'relive' them. We have to fool your brain into thinking it is in REM sleep'

'So how do we fool my brain?' I asked.

'I will wave my hand in front of your eyes and I want you to follow my hand without moving your head, just use your eyes, while you do this I want you to think of a time with Monica, the worst moment you can remember.'

Well, there were lots of memories to choose from, but I chose to focus on our first big fight where she had really hit me, the time that had caused me to be on crutches for three weeks.

Before we could do this, I had to think of a happy place, a place that I could go to feel safe and secure, I chose to imagine me being in the room where I had started to attend Buddhist meetings every now and then. It was at least a place where I felt safe and the people that were there were accepting, and it had a calmness about it.

When the therapy began, I found it impossible to hold the memory and at the same time, follow the hand. After a few times of trying, my counsellor changed tact.

'Okay, let's try this. Close your eyes and concentrate on the memory, and I will tap your knees, this has the same result. If you need to stop, just say, 'Stop.''

I was very sceptical, how could tapping my knees help PTS? But I had nothing to lose by trying, so I got comfortable and closed my eyes.

I saw Monica, her eyes black and filled with hate, I saw the rage, felt the blows, felt the fear within myself and all the time, my counsellor tapped my knees.

Then, something strange happened. I had not cried about Monica since we had broken up, but now I felt an overwhelming sadness. The tears came, not as a trickle down my cheek, but in floods. My chest jerked, and my throat wrenched out uncontrollable sobs, tears flowed freely. I had to stop the therapy, as I could not think or do anything, but cry. I felt emotion pour out of me. It was a relief, but it also hurt, it hurt my body, it hurt my brain. The scene I had envisioned was so real – ultra-real. I felt my heart break all over again.

When I had regained control, we tried again, and again, I cried and cried.

To my happy place.

When I left the session, I stopped in a quiet place on the road and put my head in my hands.

'Damn you, Monica,' I thought. *'Damn you to hell.'*

"I can survive
And I can endure
I don't even think
About her
Most of the time"

Bob Dylan

My week in between therapy sessions, was hard. The second session had brought emotions to the surface and they were manifesting themselves now, in several ways; I was crying now if I heard a song that Monica liked, or if I saw a movie that she liked. Some of the flashbacks were different now, sometimes arguments, but sometimes the voices that I heard, were her softer voice, her kind voice.

Sometimes, I would walk through my front door and hear her say, *'Babyyyyyyyy,'* like she used to do before she jumped into my arms.

Before locking the door at night, I could have sworn I saw her walking up the steps towards the flat.

I tried not to think about it, tried to occupy my mind, but it would always slip back to her. I couldn't even go to the cinema anymore, as I found myself looking for Monica in the auditorium as we had the same taste in films.

When the third session came around, I was so nervous of what would happen, and just a few seconds into the therapy I found out, as the tears came again fast and strong.

I began to doubt that the memory could ever be processed. I knew that the therapy was effective because of the emotion that was released, but processed?

My counsellor asked me questions, not only about Monica, but about how I saw myself. I told her that I felt weak and pathetic, that I saw myself as less than a man.

'Do you think those are your observations,' she asked, 'or Monica's?'

Unfortunately, how Monica saw me, and how I saw myself, had become inseparable, what Monica thought I was, I was.

I tried to imagine what normal would feel like, but it was hard to see a life without Monica controlling the way that I felt.

I needed a break, to get away, to immerse myself in new surroundings that had nothing to do with Monica or the mess I was in, just freshness of environment, and India and Nepal were the perfect solution.

I was nervous as I boarded the plane to New Delhi on November 17th, 2017. I did not know what to expect from a country I never thought I'd go to.

After eight hours I arrived in New Delhi and made my way to the hotel. It was situated in a back alley in downtown Delhi in a neighbourhood that would have not been out of place, in an Indian version of *Escape From New York*. Despite the hotel, India seemed nice, although a little pushy, the people are so poor that the desperation to sell tourists something, anything, led to 'getting in your face', an approach that most Westerners are unfamiliar with, and therefore don't like.

I liked how polite everyone was though, walking into Starbucks I was not faced with a faux smile and forced politeness, but servers who placed their hands together, gave a short bow and said, 'Namaste.'

I visited India Gate and the parliament, and the grave of Mahatma Gandhi and I also visited temples of various religious denominations. One of these temples was *Shish Ganji Gurudwara Temple* in Old Delhi. I was shocked to the point of tears by the generosity of the Sikh faith. Here, I saw a twenty-four-hour kitchen serving food to the homeless and the poor, unconditional love, for fellow human beings. My heart and mind were stunned, over the past couple of years I had seen nothing but cruelty from the woman that was supposed to have loved me, and now I witnessed strangers putting their own worries aside to see to those who had less. I had *never* seen anything so powerful.

For most of the time, Monica was pushed back in my mind. The night was different, however, with anxiety creeping in and taking control giving me sleepless nights and still voices whispered in the darkness.

After one of these sleepless nights, I headed out on the train one morning, to the city of Agra where I was to see the *Taj Mahal.*

On arrival in Agra I was met by an Indian man by the name of Farid who was to be my guide for the day. He had a kind smile and was very chatty and made me feel comfortable immediately. He did his job well, telling me the history of everything that we saw, but it was when we reached the Taj Mahal that he stepped outside of his rehearsed patter.

Farid seemed surprised, pleasantly so, at how I saw things. He loved the questions I asked, and my own insights into the most beautiful building I'd ever seen. He praised me on my critical eye and the reactions I had, my reaction being more than wonder, it was deeper than that, it was…emotional.

'I can see by the way you are that you are a very spiritual person,' he told me. 'I see tourists all the time, but very few see the Taj the way that you do.'

By the end of the trip, I felt a real bond with Farid, whether it was our mutual love of the Taj, or something deeper, something spiritual, I don't know, but we promised to stay in touch.

I felt inspired by him and inspired by the Taj Mahal. It was a symbol of devotion a declaration of deep love, it was pure and beautiful and, well, perfect.

When I returned to my hotel I felt a calm that I had not felt in a long time, and that night I slept like a baby.

"If you look around

The whole world is coming together now

Can you feel it?"

The Jackson 5

I arrived late in Kathmandu, Nepal and caught a taxi to my hotel. The Boudha Inn Meditation Center is set in a circle of hotels, shops and restaurants accessible via an arched gateway by foot. It is situated just a few short steps from the Boudhanath Stupa (a sacred building for Buddhists). This is where I was to spend the next few days.

I entered the gateway and walked in a circle trying to find my lodgings when a man walked up to me and asked me could he help. He was short with a dark brown leathery face, and he looked up at me with a mixture of kindness and curiosity. I explained that I was trying to find the Boudha Inn and he kindly walked me there.

'You have a kind face,' he said.

'Thank you,' I said warily.

My experience in India had taught me to be careful of the hard sell.

'Do you practice Buddhism?' He asked as he walked me into the hotel.

'Yes,' I said.

He stopped and looked up at me, I don't know why but I stopped too, and our eyes met. He reached up and placed a hand either side of my head and pulled me towards him and touched his forehead against mine and held it there for a few seconds. Letting go, he reached into the bag that he had hung on his shoulder and pulled out a white silk scarf. He hung the scarf around my neck.

'From my soul to yours,' he said, and with a short bow he was gone.

Stunned, I carried on into the Boudha Inn, and there I was greeted by my host.

'John,' he said.

There was no sir, no Mr James, and I didn't care.

I checked in and he showed me round, which didn't take long. The Inn is basically one corridor with rooms going off it, and at one end, there is a meditation room. It was beautiful. The space was large and spotlessly clean, there were cushions and mats piled against one wall to use for meditation and the classes that the Boudha Inn do, such as yoga and reiki. At one end of the room was a huge golden Buddha that faced you as you walked in – wonderful.

We stood talking for a while after he showed me around and I found him pleasant with an inner calm that radiated out of him.

He walked me to my room and opened the door.

'Is this okay for you?' he asked.

The room was small with a bathroom to one side and a bed on the floor – that was it.

'Perfect,' I told him.

After he had left, I put down my things and sat on the bed and cried, I don't know why, I just did.

The next morning, I awoke at 5am to the sound of chanting. I looked out of my window and saw monks and locals walking around the Stupa, their mala, or prayer beads, in hand. I watched the spectacle and it looked mesmerising, it seemed as if the people were in a trance, all they seemed to care about was that moment and nothing else seemed to matter.

I saw my host, and he asked me how my first night had been, I explained, with a twinge of embarrassment, that for some reason, I had cried.

'Why did you come to Nepal?' He asked with a nod.

'I've had a rough time,' I said without going into detail. 'I needed some...peace, I guess.'

He smiled and nodded. 'This place is special,' he said. 'We have the meditation room here, outside we have the Stupa and beneath us we have shops selling many statues of Buddha, what you felt, was the power of this place.'

He smiled, and I felt the tension come out of my shoulders and my body relax.

I decided to try the walking meditation. I went out to the Stupa and jumped in line with the monks and locals, I took off my mala, that I had been wearing for a few months now, and followed them as they walked around and around. At first, I was very self-conscious, I felt out of place and I didn't really know what to do, so I watched as I walked. I saw some touching their heads to the walls of the stupa, I saw some prostrating by lying face down on the floor, as others walked around them. They seemed so focussed on the practice, with no inhibitions.

I spent the next few minutes observing until I grew comfortable, then I began to chant:

'Om mani padme hum, om mani padme hum.' This is an ancient chant that is said to purify one's anger, ego, jealousy, desire and ignorance and promote love and forgiveness and compassion.

As time went on my chant got stronger and I felt myself falling into the moment. After a while I grew light headed and my body grew tingly and cold. I felt strange, it's hard to describe, but different somehow, lighter, less trapped in my own body, if that makes sense.

By the time I had finished my walking meditation, I felt a strange feeling. I felt…happy.

I took a shower, ate lunch and went out talking to locals and monks and enjoying the sun. In the evening, I meditated in the designated room and then I ate in the restaurant that was a floor below the Boudha Inn, and watched people walk around the Stupa in their evening prayer. By the time that I crawled into bed I realised something…I had *not* thought about Monica, all day.

"I don't need your dirty love
I don't want you touching me
I don't want your dirty love it's enough
Trying to live with the memory"

Thunder

I had booked a few trips for when I was in Nepal and one of those, was a trip to the caves in Pharping. My guide was Bijaya, and as soon as I met the man, we had an instant connection. He talked non-stop as we drove to the middle of nowhere. The city gave way to small huts and leather faced locals, with deep set eyes and warm smiles.

Bijaya told me about the surrounding area, and the history of the temples we passed, but he also imparted his theories on life and the importance of oneness of religions and of people. I listened soaking up every sentence.

'Why have you come to Nepal?' He asked, reminding me of my host at the hotel.

'I have had some problems,' I said, 'I have to come to find a new me.'

'Trying to love a negative person,' he said, 'is like standing in the river saying, 'I don't want to get wet.''

I laughed, but he was right. There was no way I could love Monica the way I wanted to, there was no way she would change to allow that to happen.

We made a stop at the foot of what seemed like a million steps. We climbed the steps to the top, my lungs close to bursting. Once there Bijaya led me to a cave. It was tiny, and we had to duck low to get inside. As we entered, I saw three monks sitting in front of an altar surrounded by candles.

Bijaya motioned for me to sit. Once seated, we meditated with the monks. I closed my eyes, I could smell the incense, I could feel the presence of the monks, feel their calm and their peace. As I sat there meditating, something happened to me, like *freeing* from the inside. I was wary at first, it felt alien to me, as had the walking meditation, but I let whatever *this was* happen, and the longer I meditated the more I could feel an inner-peace growing from my navel and filling my entire being. I was aware of my blood coursing through my veins, I was aware of the ground beneath me and the air surrounding me. I could hear my own breath in the silence of the cave, steady and rhythmic.

When we exited the cave, instinctively I knew what needed to be done. I knew how to change my life.

Bijaya and myself swapped details and vowed to stay in touch, again I had found someone inspirational to me, who showed me that life was created by me and no one else.

The next morning, I threw myself into the meditative practice of walking around the Stupa. I chanted as I held my mala to my forehead, I spun the prayer wheels, I cried for the passing of my dad. At night I engaged in the same practice, other foreign visitors stared as I passed them, the lone white man amongst the Nepalese people. I was meditating several times a day too, sitting in front of the giant golden Buddha and losing myself in a realm of peace.

My final trip of my stay was with a guide called Dipesh. He told me about the Stupa and explained the symbolism and told me of its history. He talked about the five elements of earth, water, fire, wind and space and how everything is connected, everything is one. I had never heard anyone talk like this before.

'Whose is this bag?' He said at once, pointing to my backpack.

'Mine,' I replied.

'Whose is this coat?' He asked, tugging at my sleeve.

'Mine,' I said again.

'Whose is this arm?'

'Mine.'

'And who are you?' He asked.

'John,' I replied.

'No,' he said. 'John is your name, there are millions of Johns in the world, how can John be you?' He pointed at me and said, 'This bag and this coat you said were yours, when I asked you about your arm you said, 'Mine,' as you said about your bag. Yes, your body is a possession just like your bag,' he said. 'You have this possession for a very short time, so I ask you again, who are *you*?'

I thought for the longest time, as I had never really considered it before.

'Spirit,' I said at last.

'Yes,' he said with a smile. 'You are *here*,' he pointed to the centre of my chest. 'The real *you* is here.'

Dipesh took me to a Hindu temple and there we sat on a small hill and watched a Hindu funeral. Unlike the UK there was no privacy to these matters, the body was there for all to see, wrapped in a cloth. The bodies were taken down to the river where the river water was poured into the corpses mouth and then they were cremated on a funeral pyre.

Dipesh talked about the respect that was shown to the body and to those he left behind; he spoke of living a good life, so that one may have a good death.

'Why did you come to Nepal?' He asked.

Was it so unusual? Everyone wanted to know why I was here.

I told him as I had told the others, without going into detail, 'I have been through some things.'

'Think of walking,' he said. 'To walk you have to abandon the previous step, if you do not then you will stand still forever. To walk you have to abandon that step, you have to leave things behind to move forward.'

He was so right, I had been standing in the same spot for months now, refusing to abandon my step, I identified with the past and had been unable or afraid to take a step forward.

My mind was full of ideas, and my heart full of hope, as my stay in the magical city of Kathmandu drew to a close.

On the morning of my departure, I left my hotel and I walked to the arched gate entrance and turned back, looking up at the Boudhanath Stupa. I stood for a moment in silence, then I put my hands together and bowed.

'Namaste,' I said quietly.

"Raindrops keep falling on my head

But that doesn't mean my eyes

will soon be turning red

Crying's not for me, cause

I'm never gonna stop the rain by complaining"

B J Thomas

I had met three inspirational men, in fact, the whole country had inspired me. It was like I'd been walking around with severe cataracts for years, and now Nepal had brushed them aside and given me a new vision.

I was now meditating twice a day, and I would join the locals and monks in their walking meditation two or three times a day. The walking meditation had taught me that, to achieve peace, I needed to be present, to focus on what is *now,* rather than the past, or even, the future.

When I returned to England, I was reborn. I knew what I had to do, and I knew the way I had to live my life. It was true that there was little help for male victims of abuse and I knew that I had to highlight that somehow, although how to go about that, eluded me at the time.

I threw away my medication and instead I found a new medicine – compassion.

I began to work as a volunteer helping the homeless, I gave others what I wished for myself. I began to hungrily read the writings of Eckhart Tolle and Michael Singer. I began to understand that the past does not exist, only in my own mind and therefore Monica had not tortured my head for the last nine months, *I* had. I was in control of my inner world and only I can allow negativity in. Monica had left me back in April so how could she possibly hurt me since then?

I understood that the little voice in my head, that had been so destructive with its constant chattering was not *me*, not the real me, it was my ego, and he loved negative thinking and ill feeling. But the real me was, as Dipesh had said, deep inside, and it was time to bring the real me out into the open.

The next therapy session I had I was excited. I showered my counsellor with stories of Nepal and the people I'd met there and how amazing I felt, how the world seemed different somehow.

I could see that she was pleased but cautious, was this a phase, the excitement of being away? She told me that she was happy for me, but she'd like to see me again to see how I was, I agreed, but that next meeting was to be my final one.

'I don't know what happened to you over there,' she said, 'but I don't think you need me anymore.'

I forgave Monica, too, not just 'didn't care', but really forgave her. I even wrote her a letter, apologising for anything I might have done to upset her, telling her I was happy and wishing her happiness, health and peace. I didn't mention what she did, I didn't need to, it didn't matter at all, the letter was purely to give me closure, to offer spiritual love.

Even now, I think about her every now and then and even miss stroking her back at night, or the kiss before she went to work, the excited greeting when I came home, but the person I loved and still love, does not exist, it's an illusion and I know that.

My friends began to send me messages in response to my posts on Facebook and Instagram, they loved my new positive approach, my happiness made them happy; positivity is really infectious, that's not just blah blah, it really is. I began to help others overcome their blues, passing on what I had learned for myself, some embraced it, some did not, but I had learned that when one identifies with misery it's hard to let go, it becomes a piece of you.

When I visited my mum, she knew instantly that there was something different.

'Where's John gone?' She said, 'You've changed so much. You're so calm and quiet.'

That calm and quiet is called *stillness* and was, and still is, the corner stone of my life. Another thing that became a huge part of my life was acceptance; acceptance of the imperfect me, acceptance that people are who they are, good or bad, and acceptance of what is. If something bad happens, can I change it? If not, then it is what it is – cause I'm never gonna stop the rain by complaining.

Namaste

Some people have asked me why I wrote this book and my answer is simple – because it needed to be written. As I said at the beginning, I don't want sympathy or empathy, I don't want to be seen as a victim and I don't want these things because, through this book, I have a voice, there are thousands, possibly millions of men out there who do not.

15% of men between the ages of 16 and 59 have experienced some kind of domestic abuse in their life, that's the equivalent of 2.4 million men. Between 2016 and 2017 4.3% of men reported domestic abuse, that is over 700,000 men. Imagine the statistics without the stigma, without the shame that a lot of men feel, how high would that number be if every case was reported? In 2016/2017 13 men were murdered as a result of domestic violence, yet sadly, men are three times less likely to report abuse than women.

I don't want to preach, that is not my intention, but the disparity needs to be addressed. More services, such as dedicated helplines, need to be put into place. Since writing this book, I have discovered more than the Men's Advice Line that offer help, but they are not in the spotlight as women's charities are. I am not insinuating that men are more important than women, but the disparity between the two genders *is* important.

Police really need better training, and male victims of domestic violence *really need* to be heard without fear of prejudice. They need to understand the abused individual, understand that abuse is a complex matter and understand that emotional and psychological abuse is as, if not more, destructive than physical violence. I am sure that there are many fine officers out there who are sympathetic and empathic, but this needs to be across the board.

My own understanding has grown since my experience. I have come across terms such as 'gaslighting' – *manipulate someone psychologically until they doubt their own reality* – and gained a deeper understanding of 'Stockholm Syndrome' in abuse victims, which makes it difficult to leave their abuser. I have read about 'Narcissistic Personality Disorder' and 'Borderline Personality Disorder'. But even with all this gained knowledge, I will still never understand why I stayed, why I loved Monica as much as I did after suffering so much.

Domestic violence by women is a reality and this should not, must not, be ignored. Abuse is evil and destructive whether the victim be a man, a woman or a child, but there needs to be a balance here.

We need to make it safe and supportive for men to speak out, change our ideas of what a *man* is. I see it already with male victims of sexual abuse coming forward and speaking out, now *more* needs to be done.

I have been the butt of jokes, after my experience with Monica, people telling me to stop complaining and to *get over it*. This is the exact counter-productive and, let's be honest, ignorant attitude that holds men back from speaking out. So, the abusers are to blame, yes, but in a way, we are all to blame, all of our societal stereotypes and non-forward-thinking attitudes.

It's time to STOP.

It's time to SPEAK OUT.

Namaste

Part 2:

I would like to share two messages I received after I returned to England, one from Farid and one from Bijaya whom I met in India and Nepal respectively:

"Thank you so much for remembering us and taking you around my city was a privilege to me and I got to learn a lot....it is about the ability of finding oneself out of oneself and you, I think, are blessed with that sense...therefore all credit goes to you, John...thanks and regards"

Farid

"Sadhu! Sadhu

There is a magnet in our heart that will attract true friend, that magnet is unselfishness, thinking of others first: good thinking to live for others as much as we can. If we have all this attitude then others will live for us................

You are this type. Wish success on your quest.

Bijaya

These two comments mean the world to me and I will be forever grateful to Bijaya, Farid and Dipesh for their kindness, their generosity and their wisdom.

Despite the lack of resources for male victims of domestic violence, changing your life yourself can help greatly. It is not easy to change, and in some respects, I see myself as lucky. Many people suffer abuse every day, and in a lot of cases it leaves permanent scars physically, psychologically and emotionally, however, there is light out there, there is hope, a new life beyond the hitting and humiliation, beyond the controlling behaviour of others.

The past truly does not exist except in one's own mind.

Sit and think, *'What time am I in?'*

You are in the *Now*, the present.

Wait an hour and ask yourself, *'What time am I in now?'*

The answer will be the same. You do not live in any other time other than the present, so make the most of it. If you are identifying with the past or dreaming of the future, then you are missing so much that is around you.

This is not some mystical mumbo jumbo, this is how things are. If one can live in the *Now*, be totally conscious in the present moment, then nothing else matters.

I have been lucky enough to change my life, to find an inner peace and happiness, lucky enough to be able to have my voice via this book, and I am grateful for that.

I hope my story has, not only shown you an insight into abuse and how it can affect every aspect of your life, but also shown you how to live in the aftermath. *You* are in control of *you*, don't let anyone tell you different.

Peace.

"Risin' up back on the street
Did my time, took my chances
Went the distance, now I'm back on my feet
Just a man and his will to survive"

Survivor

Helplines

Men's Advice Line

www.mensadviceline.org.uk

Tel: 0808 801 0327

e-mail: infor@mensadviceline.org.uk

Victim Support

www.victimsupport.org.uk

Supportline: 080816 89111

ManKind Initiative

www.mankind.org,uk

Tel: 01823 334244

Refuge

www.refuge.org.uk

Tel: 0808 2000 247

helpline@refuge.org.uk

Recommended reading

The Power of Now by Eckhart Tolle
(Hodder & Stoughton, 1999)

A New Earth by Eckhart Tolle (Penguin Books, 2016)

The Untethered Soul: The Journey Beyond Yourself
by Michael Singer (New Harbinger, 2007)

How to See Yourself As You Really Are
by Dalai Lama (Rider Publishing, 2008)

The Art of Happiness by Dalai Lama
(Hodder Paperbacks, 1999)

I Hate You, Don't Leave Me by
Jerold.J., MD Kresisman and Hal Straus
(Perigee, 2011)

Contact and Social Media for John James Author

Email: fromthedarknessbook@gmail.com

Website: www.fromthedarknessbook.co.uk

Facebook: JohnJamesAuthor
https://www.facebook.com/JohnJamesAuthor

Twitter: FTDbook
https://www.twitter.com/FTDbook

Instagram: fromthedarknessbook
https://www.instagram.com/fromthedarknessbook

YouTube: John James From The Darkness
https://www.youtube.com/channel/UCF4L5lto0zMN1nyoOBeoeOQ

Soundcloud: John James From The Darkness
https://soundcloud.com/jj-66

Made in the USA
Las Vegas, NV
03 August 2022